# A BANQUET ON A BUDGET

Judy Ridgway

ROBINSON

ROBINSON

First published in Great Britain in 2016 by Robinson

Copyright © Judy Ridgway, 2016

1 3 5 7 9 10 8 6 4 2

A CIP catalogue record for this book
is available from the British Library.

ISBN: 978-1-47213-658-9 (paperback)

Typeset by Basement Press, Glaisdale
Printed and bound by CPI Group (UK) Ltd, Croydon, CR0 4YY

Papers used by Robinson are from well-managed forests and other
responsible sources.

MIX
Paper from
responsible sources
FSC
www.fsc.org    FSC® C104740

Robinson
is an imprint of
Little, Brown Book Group
Carmelite House
50 Victoria Embankment
London EC4Y 0DZ

An Hachette UK Company
www.hachette.co.uk

www.littlebrown.co.uk

**Judy Ridgway** is a very experienced cookery writer, with extensive media contacts and first-hand experience of radio and TV. She has more than 60 books to her name, including *Running Your Own Catering Company*, *Running Your Own Wine Bar* and *Wining and Dining at Home*. She also co-wrote *The Catering Management Handbook* with her brother Brian Ridgway, who at the time was operations director for the Thistle group of hotels.

Judy ran a small catering company called London Cooks Ltd. Parties of all kinds, including weddings, featured prominently in the work of the company and her experiences at that time have contributed greatly to the writing of this book.

# CONTENTS

# INTRODUCTION

The date has been set and the planning has started. So what about the catering? 'Why not do it ourselves?' someone suggests. It seems a perfectly straightforward idea and, indeed, many people do carry it through very successfully.

Before you make the final decision, you should give some thought to what is involved. On the plus side, you will certainly save a good deal of money and you will also have the satisfaction of providing your family and friends with the best that home-cooking can offer. The party will remain a very personal affair without the formality of outside caterers.

On the minus side, the work involved can be quite onerous, and if you have a small kitchen you will need quite a lot of ingenuity to work out the logistics of cooking for a large number of people. Thought will certainly need to be given as to who will mastermind the overall plan and who will carry out all the work. If Mum is a good cook and there is an extended family of brothers and sisters or aunts and uncles who can lend a hand, it will probably be a lot easier than if you do not have many relatives or friends to call upon. However, you can always compromise by doing the cooking yourself and hiring waiting staff for the event itself.

If the decision is taken to cater for yourselves, I hope this book will help you to plan the event and to carry out all the tasks involved with the minimum of effort. I have tried to include all the hints and tips I have come across, both in talking to other people and in catering for quite a few events myself when I was running my own catering company, London Cooks Ltd.

**NOTE**
I usually use large eggs, rather than medium.

# SETTING THE SCENE
# FOR YOUR SPECIAL PARTY

There is no single blueprint for successful party food. Canapés and drinks can work just as well as a finger buffet or a sit-down meal. The choice is entirely yours and will depend on such factors as the number of guests you plan to invite, the size of your budget and the availability of a suitable venue.

But before you can sensibly make the choice and start to plan, you will need to have the answers to a few basic questions.

## HOW MUCH CAN YOU AFFORD TO SPEND?
The answer to this question will affect your replies to many of the other questions and will, of course, influence the final plan.

## WHEN IS THE EVENT TO BE?
What time of the year will it take place and how much time will you have in hand to put your plans into effect? What time of the day will it be?

## HOW MANY PEOPLE WILL YOU INVITE?
If you are planning a wedding, you will need to look at the proportion of family and friends on both sides. Whether you are celebrating an anniversary or birthday, organising a special party

for Christmas or just planning a great get-together you will still need to consider the numbers.

## DO YOU HAVE SUFFICIENT SPACE TO HOLD THE RECEPTION AT HOME?

Will you be able to use the garden? Is the house large enough to hold everyone if the weather is bad?

## WHAT TYPE OF RECEPTION WOULD YOU PREFER?

Are you happy to have everyone standing up for canapés or finger food, or would you prefer a sit-down buffet or formal meal?

## HOW MANY PEOPLE WILL YOU BE ABLE TO ROPE IN TO HELP WITH ALL THE PREPARATION?

## WILL YOU NEED OUTSIDE HELP?

If you are planning a wedding reception, the prospective bride and groom will need to get together with their parents or whoever is going to host the wedding to help in answering these questions. Once you have worked through them all and have agreed answers between those most closely concerned, you will be well on the way to having a good idea of what you hope to achieve.

## POSSIBLE CATERING RECEPTION SCENARIOS

- Fork buffet for 40 at home, using the living room and hall.
- Canapés and drinks for 100, in a local hall.
- Sit-down meal for 14, using the living room at home.
- Finger buffet for 50 with a marquee in the garden.
- Fork buffet for 60 in a local clubhouse.

## THE PLAN

Whatever type of event you decide to have, the key to success lies in working out a good plan of campaign. This will take in the guest list, details of the menu and the drinks, and a timetable to cover shopping and preparation, as well as a checklist for the day itself.

If the party is to be held at your home, it is also a good idea to include a list of thoughtful touches you could add around the house. This might include combs in the bedrooms or bathroom and a list of taxi numbers by the phone, anything which adds to the comfort and enjoyment of your guests.

The more detailed your plan, the less likelihood there is of anything going wrong and the easier it will be for the host and hostess to enjoy the party along with their guests.

Use the master checklist provided below to help you put together your plan, and read the following general notes on the various sections of the plan. Further helpful information on specific types of catering will be found within the chapters that follow.

## MASTER CHECKLIST

### WELL IN ADVANCE
- Set the date and send out the invitations; keep a record of the replies.
- Decide upon and, if necessary, book the venue.
- Plan the drinks and the menu.
- Book waiters or waitresses or start to organise your family and friends.
- Arrange to hire glasses, tablecloths and platters and any other equipment you will need.
- Order or make the cake for an anniversary or wedding.

## ONE MONTH OR SO BEFORE

- Start the shopping and order the drinks.
- Start advance preparation.
- Order flowers and find out where to buy ice.
- Plan the method of transport to a venue away from home, with a fallback plan in case the transport breaks down.

## ONE WEEK BEFORE

- Prepare a plan of action for the morning of the party.
- Finish decorating the cake, if necessary.
- Complete advance preparation and write out a final shopping list.
- Shop for non-perishable items.

## THE DAY BEFORE

- Finish off any perishable shopping.
- Finish all advance preparation.
- Make extra ice if you are not planning to buy it.
- Organise the rooms to be used if you are catering at home, and clear them of furniture and breakable ornaments.

## ON THE DAY

- Decorate the room and the tables.
- Chill the white wine.
- Work through the preparation plan.
- Organise the house.

# TIMING

The timing of the party can affect the planning. For example, you may want to serve rather different food for a lunchtime barbecue than for an evening dinner. You might also want to consider an afternoon tea party or an early-evening drinks party. The choice may also depend on how far the guests have to travel to the event and the average age of the guests. If friends have travelled a long way they will need more to eat than just a canapé or two, and older guests may often prefer to eat in the middle of the day and to eat sitting down.

If you are planning a wedding reception, the timing may well be dictated by the availability of the church or the registry office. The most popular times for weddings are around midday with a late lunchtime reception, or mid-afternoon, with a reception in the early evening.

The latter arrangement offers whoever is catering more time on the day to prepare and still get to the wedding ceremony. One family I know, arranged the latest ceremony they could, which was at 5 p.m. The reception was then set for 7.30 p.m. in the evening.

# THE INVITATIONS

It is all too easy for any guest list to escalate in the enthusiasm of early planning. This is particularly true for a wedding. When two families' lists have to be put together the result can be very long indeed. This is fine if there is unlimited space and no cash problems, but most people have to watch what they are spending and so the budget can sometimes be quite tight. If so, should you limit the guests to relatives and very close family friends? Should the bride and groom be able to invite all their young friends and forget about Great-Aunt Mary? What happens if the bridegroom has an extended family and the bride has only a couple of relatives? These questions often cause a good deal of conflict and need to be discussed in a calm and friendly atmosphere.

The size of the final guest list will probably affect the type of catering you decide to have. A canapés and drinks party where everyone stands up will allow you to entertain rather more people in a given space than a sit-down buffet would allow.

The invitations will, of course, state the time of the event, but they should also give some indication of the type of food to be served. If it is to be a canapés and drinks reception, do make this clear on the invitation. Guests who have had to travel some distance will then be able to make arrangements to eat a full meal either before or after the reception.

## THE VENUE

The easiest place to hold any kind of self-catered party is in your own home. The food preparation can take place in your own familiar kitchen and you will not have far to carry it to the serving tables.

### AT HOME

Depending upon the numbers you are planning to invite, you might decide to use the living room alone, or, if you have more rooms, the whole of the downstairs area including the hall, leaving the bedrooms for any display of presents and for coats and hats. The latter will be particularly important if it is wintertime or the weather is bad.

If it is a summer party, you might be able to make use of the garden, but weather can be rather unpredictable and unless you have the space to hold a marquee, you must be sure there is room for everyone to retreat to the house.

## OUTSIDE VENUE

If your house or, in the case of a wedding, the bride or bridegroom's family home, is too small, you may be able to arrange the use of a friend or relative's house. But do remember that this will need to be cleaned and fully tidied up afterwards more quickly than your own home.

Outside venues will often hold more people, but many of them either do not have kitchen facilities, or they are tied to the use of a specific caterer and so you cannot do your own catering.

If you don't know of a local venue, start by checking local church, parish and village halls. Public buildings such as town halls, baths and libraries may also have rooms for hire. Talk to your local events photographer; he or she may well be aware of local venues through their work.

Other ideas include sports clubhouses or your old school premises. You could even hire a large boat on the river. However, do remember to check on the kitchen facilities; it really is very difficult to bring absolutely everything in with you. There must at least be running hot and cold water and an electric point or two!

In fact, you will probably need rather more equipment than this. Here's a checklist to use when visiting the venue for the first time:

## KITCHEN AND WORKING AREA

• How much working surface is there? If there is not much, is there room to put up a trestle table?

9

- What cooking appliances are available and how do they work?
- Are there sufficient power points to use electric appliances such a food processors and whisks?
- Is there a fridge to chill the food and wine?
- Is there a second sink for chilling wine? If not, could you use a dustbin?
- Is there enough room to wash-up or should you use disposable plates?

## RECEPTION ROOM

- Is there room for tables and chairs, or must it be a stand-up event?
- Where will the buffet and drinks tables go?
- If it is a formal event, where will the guests be received?
- Where will the cake go?
- What is the colour scheme? You may want to colour-coordinate flowers, napkins and candles.
- Where are the toilets situated? This is useful information to pass on to the waiting staff, who will then be able to direct guests.

# THE FOOD AND DRINK

## THE MENU

The choice of menu will obviously be heavily influenced by the style of reception you have chosen to adopt. Cold roast beef or turkey is difficult to eat with a fork alone and so should be reserved for sit-down buffets or full-scale sit-down meals. Mini-quiches and sausage rolls, on the other hand, make excellent finger food.

## COSTINGS

The cost will also be another important factor. If it is a wedding or a very special anniversary you will probably be prepared to spend a little more than you would for a birthday party. It really is important not to cut corners. It is far better to invite fewer people than to try to impress with a large event and serve inferior food and wine. You will end up not impressing anyone this way.

If the budget is really tight, you can use small quantities of exotic or expensive ingredients to dress things up and create a feeling of luxury from first-class presentation. The imaginative use of readily available ingredients can also add interest to an economical spread. It also makes sense to mix expensive items, such as smoked salmon or scampi, with more economical ingredients like eggs or cheese.

## TIMINGS

One factor often forgotten when putting the menu together is the time that each item takes to prepare. A menu featuring pies, flans and terrines will take much longer to prepare than cold cuts and salads.

## HOW MUCH?

The quantities involved could also affect the final choice of menu. Is your oven large enough to take a 9kg turkey and have you enough 25cm flan cases to make four large strawberry tarts? Of course you may decide to cut the workload or solve the equipment problem by buying in most of the food ready-made. The drawback with this approach is that it will put up the cost quite considerably.

*Some dishes are always popular. Poached salmon and strawberries is a summer party combination of which people rarely tire. Coronation or Celebration Chicken Salad is another favourite, and smoked salmon in any form disappears off the plate at a rate of knots!*

One of the secrets of successful menu planning is that the variety of food and courses on offer should be balanced. It is no good, for example, selecting an array of attractive and unusual dishes if they all have a similar base.

For canapés and finger food, aim at a mix of bread, pastry and vegetable-based items, rather than all bread-based. Make sure there is not a heavy reliance on pastry in a finger buffet and check that your fork buffet does not have a rich and creamy main course followed by a cream-based dessert. Don't serve seafood as a starter if the main course is fish and avoid too many salads which look very similar on a cold buffet.

# QUANTITIES

This is always a tricky question. You do not want to run out of food, nor do you want to over-cater and waste your money. However, the temptation to make just a little more is often overwhelming.

The answer is to sit down and work out the quantities from smaller numbers within your experience. You know how much is required for four, six, eight, even ten or twelve people. So start doubling up, taking a little of the total amounts at twenty-five, fifty, seventy-five and a hundred to make allowances for any overestimating you probably did at the beginning. A small amount left over or served as a second helping to ten people will have grown to at least two or three portions for twenty-five people, and so on.

Doubling quantities works reasonably well for most recipes, but sometimes certain ingredients may not need to be increased quite as much as others. This applies particularly to the liquid element in casseroles and stews; also to spices and other strongly flavoured ingredients.

Sometimes it helps to visualise what the food will look like on the plate. In this way you can decide how many people a 25cm flan will serve or how many items to include in a finger buffet.

# ADVANCE PREPARATION

One of the ways of coping with the amount of cooking which needs to be done is to prepare it gradually over the days or even weeks before the event and to store it in the fridge or freezer.

It is important here to decide which items on your chosen menu will freeze well and those that will not. Of course, some dishes may be semi-prepared and finished off at a later date. Quiches and flans, for example, tend to go a little soggy if they are frozen. However, the pastry cases and the fillings can be prepared and the former cooked; they can then be frozen separately and will then only need to be thawed, put together and baked on the day.

Sort out the dishes you are planning to make according to the ease of storage. Cook the freezable ones first, then the ones that can be refrigerated, and lastly those which need to be stored in tins or in the open larder.

Don't forget that cooked pastry does not survive well in the fridge, that some salad items, such as grated carrots, can last longer if coated with oil and that butter, cheeses, ice-cream and sorbets will need to be taken out of the fridge or freezer in good time to soften up.

As an example, here is a detailed advance preparation plan for the Fork Buffet Menu 5 (see page 167). The plans included in each section are not quite as detailed as this one and each will also depend on your own particular circumstances, equipment, size of freezer, etc.

## ONE TO TWO WEEKS BEFORE THE RECEPTION
- Prepare, cook and freeze the Pork and Herb Terrine
- Make and freeze the Orange Cassata Bombe

## TWO DAYS BEFORE THE RECEPTION
- Roast the gammon and store in the fridge

## THE DAY BEFORE THE RECEPTION
- Prepare the Seafood Mousse
- Make the Yorkshire Curd Tarts
- Cook the rice for the Fruity Rice Salad and store in a cool place

- Roast the vegetables for the Mediterranean Roasted Vegetable Salad and store in a cool place

## PRESENTATION

Clever presentation can transform a good buffet into a superlative one and it is well worth giving some thought to this aspect of the reception.

One of the most stunning cold buffets I have ever seen was all arranged on glass mirrors with tiny flowers made from radishes, button mushrooms, spring onions, carrots and courgettes. This may be a bit ambitious for most of us, but a lot can be done to make food look even more attractive.

Starting with the food itself, it's worth making sure that it is naturally colourful and attractive. Balance dark casseroles with colourful vegetable mixes and use garnishes to set off cold meats and fish.

### CANAPÉS

Canapé food in particular needs finishing off with some decoration before it begins to look appetising. Arranging the trays needs careful thought, too. A tray of nothing but vol-au-vents or liver pâté canapés will lack colour and life. However, if you mix five or six different items on a tray and arrange them in patterns such as diagonals or circles, they will look much more interesting. Simple canapés can be made to look really stunning if they are served on a mirror.

### FINGER FOOD

Finger food such as cocktail sausages, meatballs or devils on horseback will look much more attractive if they are liberally sprinkled with freshly chopped herbs or are served on a bed of interesting leaves, or alternatively, on sprouted alfalfa or boxed cress.

Bring trays of food to life with colourful garnishes, such as slices of orange with watercress, tomato flowers with shredded lettuce, or mixed pepper rings with parsley.

## GARNISHES FOR COLD DISHES

- Kumquats or cherry tomatoes cut in half with a crenelated pattern
- Radishes, spring onions or celery sticks cut into flower shapes
- Pea shoots or small bean sprouts
- Small bunches of fresh herbs
- Wedges, twists or butterflies of lemon, orange and lime
- Sliced kiwifruit or star fruit
- Pomegranate seeds

A centrepiece on a tray will also look most attractive. Try a cushion of watercress studded with flower heads or a small bowl of crushed ice, prawns in their shells and lemon wedges.

## THE TABLE

Buffet tables rely very much on a colourful array of food, and cold hams, turkey and chicken can be decorated with a cold sauce or with aspic. Make up pretty designs using bay leaves, black, pink and green peppercorns, sliced stuffed olives and gherkin fans.

The food on a buffet table and at a formal sit-down meal looks its best against a white background and it is well worth hiring large linen tablecloths along with cutlery and crockery.

Flowers offer the simplest way of enlivening the table, but these should be placed at the end rather than in the middle of a buffet table. This is important because they can hinder the easy flow of people around the buffet table. Flowers on a formal table should be kept low so that diners can see each other over the top of them.

Colour coordinated napkins and candles work well and you might also consider decorating the buffet table with ribbons. If it is well done, it can look very attractive. This might be a job you could hand over to a talented member of your family.

## HEALTH AND SAFETY

As this is a private party you do not need to have your kitchen inspected and approved by the local Health and Safety Department as you would if you were to set up a business catering from home. However, kitchen hygiene is important and it makes sense to take as much care as possible as you do not want any of your guests coming down with any kind of stomach upset or food poisoning.

Give the kitchen a good scrub down before you start and make sure that the work surfaces, the fridge and the freezer are absolutely clean. Keep raw meat well away from prepared foods. Check that your fridge and freezer temperatures are correct: the fridge should be set at 6°C and the freezer at -18°C.

Cooked meat and fish dishes, sauces and soups should be frozen as quickly as possible after they are cooked. Do not leave them hanging around in a warm kitchen. Take care, too, when you are thawing food. If possible, thaw meat and fish dishes in the fridge.

## THE DRINKS

It is possible to offer a full bar at your party, but I do not recommend this because it can be extremely expensive both in terms of the drinks and the staff.

A full bar entails supplies of four or five spirits, vermouth, sherry, red and white wine and beer. You will also need a good stock of soft drinks and mixers. Running such a bar can be a full-time job and you will still need helpers to distribute the drinks and serve the food.

## CHOOSING WINE

A much better idea is to serve only wine and soft drinks. If you really plan to push the boat out, you could serve champagne throughout. A more economical alternative is to serve one of the many good French sparkling wines now on the market, such as Saumur, Crémant de Bourgogne, Blanquette de Limoux or Clairette de Die; a cava from Spain; or a sweet Asti Spumante from Italy. Australia also offers some very reasonable sparkling wines.

It is also perfectly acceptable to offer a choice of red or white wine with a single glass of champagne or sparkling wine to accompany the desserts or the toasts, and this could be quite a saving on the budget.

Good but reasonable white wines are some of the French vins de pays, such as vin de pays d'Oc or Côte du Gascoigne, Spanish white Rioja, Italian Pinot Grigio, Portuguese Vinho Verde or a sweeter German Niersteiner or Mosel wine. Slightly more expensive are French Chablis and Sauvignon or New World Sauvignon and Chardonnay.

Red wine choices also include the range of French vins de pays or Beaujolais Villages, a good Italian Valpolicella, Argentinian or Bulgarian Merlot or, more expensively, a red Rioja, a French claret or an Australian Cabernet Sauvignon.

Wine can usually be bought on a supply and return basis. In this way you can be sure you will not run out. Nor will you be left with a case or more of wine to drink up.

## SERVING WINE

Wine should be served at the correct temperature and this means chilling white wine and champagne. Ideally, an hour in the fridge will bring the wine to the correct temperature. However, the fridge will probably be full of food, so the wine will have to be chilled in some other way.

The answer is to buy plenty of bags of ice and to fill buckets, a clean dustbin or even the bath with the bottles and the ice. Add some water and the wine will chill even more easily. Make sure that the bins are topped with more wine and fresh ice as the bottles are removed for serving.

Red wine should be served at room temperature, but this does not mean at the temperature of a centrally heated home or a hot summer's day. Try to store it in a reasonably cool place and bring into the reception when it's needed.

## THE CAKE

Successful cake-making and decorating really does require a degree of skill, so if you are not sure that you can cope with the cake, you would be well advised to go to a specialist cake-maker to have one made. Alternatively, you could make the cake yourself, then have it professionally decorated.

You will usually find quite a few cake-makers and decorators advertised in the local newspapers, or you might also ask your local wedding photographer if he or she can recommend someone. After all, they probably photograph a fair number of wedding cakes as part of the job.

Whether you decide to order a cake or go ahead and make your own, here's a checklist to help you make sure it's a success.

- Do you want a traditional fruit-based wedding or birthday cake, or are you going to go for a sponge base – or even something quite different, such as a French profiterole mountain?
- If you are planning a traditional wedding cake, how many tiers, if any, will you make? Will the bride want to keep the top tier for a possible christening? If so, you should warn her that after a while the oil from the marzipan will start to discolour the icing and the cake may need to be re-iced.
- What sort of icing and decoration would you like to have? If it's a wedding cake, are you going to go for colour and, if so, do you have a piece of material from the bridesmaid's dress or other reference to guide the cake-maker? If it's an anniversary or birthday cake, will you go for traditional decoration or for a theme relevant to the person or the event?
- How far will you have to transport the cake to the reception and does it have to be moved again once it has been delivered? The answers to these questions could prohibit the use of lace collars, for example, which are very fragile indeed.
- If you are making your own cake, do you need to beg, borrow or buy large cake tins or decorating material?

## DISTRIBUTING THE WEDDING CAKE

At a wedding the cake is served after its ceremonial cutting. It is quite a pretty idea to distribute it in baskets lined with napkins the same colour as those being handed out. Remember to buy boxes in which to send pieces to absent friends.

# ORGANISING HELP
# AND EQUIPMENT

A look at the final menu and the number of guests will soon tell you if you can really cope on your own or whether you need extra help and, if the answer is yes, then you will need to get it lined up as soon as possible.

## RECRUITING HELP FROM FRIENDS
## AND FAMILY

Friends and family are usually more than willing to offer help, but organising these offers to the best advantage is not always so easy. First of all you need to establish that an offer is really genuine and, if it is, exactly how much help is being offered. It is better to have fewer helpers who are prepared to put in some real time than a hoard of people who do not really want to do very much.

One way of organising your helpers is to detail each one to produce a particular dish or specific quantity of x or y. One very successful buffet I attended was produced by six or seven members of the family who were each contracted to roast the meat, make the pavlovas, prepare the salads and so on, and deliver them to the venue on the day. This is fine if you know that everyone is both reliable and good at cooking.

## ORGANISING THE HELP

If you are not so sure of your helpers' ability or reliability, it may be better to keep the cooking under your own supervision and ask for help at home. If you do this you should make sure that all your helpers know you are in charge and that things will be done your way. The best help is actually in carrying out all the not-so-nice preparation such as peeling potatoes, chopping vegetables, cooking rice and the like. This then leaves you free to make the special dishes yourself.

If there is to be a happy atmosphere in the kitchen, it is important that everyone knows exactly what you want them to do. So do make your requests as clear as possible. It's no good complaining that the canapés have been topped with olives when you wanted fresh herbs if your helper had not understood this at the beginning.

Help will probably be needed both in advance and on the day. In addition to help in the kitchen, you will need people to serve or hand round the food and drinks, and you may decide to hire people to do this. If not, it's worth thinking about asking a few of the younger guests to help out. Here again, everyone needs to be clearly briefed on what you are expecting them to do.

## HIRING STAFF

If you decide not to try to press-gang your friends and relatives into the kitchen but think that you will still need some help, there are a number of outside agencies you can call on.

The first step is to decide exactly what kind of help you require and how skilled it needs to be. I have found that unskilled help is best in the kitchen. That way you get all the laborious and dirty jobs done, plus the washing up, leaving you free to concentrate on the real cooking and on the presentation.

## UNSKILLED STAFF

Unskilled kitchen help can be obtained from any general or casual employment agency. Find out exactly what the hourly rates are and then work out how much help you will need with the advance preparation and how much you will need on the day. Remember that even if you want to see to all the food yourself, you may still want someone to wash up. Incidentally, it can be a good idea to get someone to wash up anyway. You and your friends will not feel like clearing up in your party clothes!

## PROFESSIONAL STAFF

Professional help is often preferable in the service area. A really good waitress or butler can be worth their weight in gold. They will know exactly what to do, having been involved in many more events and weddings than you are likely to have been! An experienced waitress can also help to make sure the food is evenly distributed among the guests and that the first to arrive at a buffet do not clear the lot!

Waiters, waitresses and butlers usually work on an hourly basis and you will be asked to sign a timesheet at the end of the contracted time. A butler will cost more than an ordinary waiter, but it is well worth employing one if you are having quite a large reception. He or she will take over the briefing and overseeing of the other waiting staff and should ensure that your reception runs like clockwork. If there is a problem at any stage, a butler will spot this and either deal with it themselves or pull staff in from another area to help out.

## HOW MANY?

Allow two members of staff for each of these scenarios:

- Canapés and drinks for 20–25 guests
- Finger buffet for 30–35 guests
- Fork buffet for 25
- Sit-down meal for 16

## FINDING STAFF

Waiting staff are usually to be found through specialist agencies dealing only with catering staff. Have a look in your local Yellow Pages or Thomson Local directories under 'Catering Staff Agencies'. You may also find freelance staff advertising their services in the Jobs Wanted section of the local paper.

## PAYING STAFF

Waiters, waitresses and butlers are usually paid by the hour. So check the rates and remember that weekend work is often one and a half to two times the week-time rate. Some agencies like you to sign their timesheets and will then send you an invoice. Others prefer you to pay the staff on the spot. If the work has been carried out particularly well you may want to tip over and above the agreed rate. Give this direct to the staff concerned, regardless of whether you are paying by invoice or direct.

Waiting staff do not always have their own transport, so you may also need to budget for a taxi to and from inaccessible venues, or arrange for them to be picked up and returned to a central point such as the local railway station.

# HIRING EQUIPMENT

Some of the arrangements for your party could necessitate outside involvement. You may want to hire a marquee, for example, and hire crockery, cutlery and glasses or engage staff. If so, you should get on with these items as soon as possible after finalising your plans. This is even more important if the event is a wedding. May to July, for example, is the 'high season' for weddings. Staff get booked up way in advance and it has been known for equipment hire companies to run out of gilt chairs and attractive crockery.

## MARQUEES

A marquee in the garden is an excellent way of extending the space available for the reception and it can work particularly well if it is possible to place it close to a set of French windows.

A marquee can be quite plain and functional and if you are prepared to risk the weather, a small one can be set up simply to hold the buffet table and drinks. Part of it can also be used to extend the preparation space for a cold buffet. More elaborate marquees can be hired with pretty linings and other decorative features.

The problem with hiring a marquee is that it can be very expensive. It will also need to be booked well in advance. However, if you do decide to go ahead and have a marquee, here are some points to consider:

- Will the sides of the marquee open up if the day is a really hot one?
- What is to be provided in the way of a floor, or is your lawn to take the full load?
- Will it be necessary to lay on some power for electric points and lighting?

• How will the food be moved from the kitchen to the marquee and where is the washing-up to be done?

Equipment requirements fall broadly into three categories: kitchen, reception and electrical.

## KITCHEN EQUIPMENT

Most of the problems here concern the size and quantity of the food to be prepared. Is your oven large enough to take a really large roast and, if not, can you use a neighbour's larger oven? Do you have pans that are large enough to cook sufficient new potatoes, rice or pasta for 60 people? Do you have a microwave oven for heating up cocktail canapés or can you borrow one?

Catering equipment hire companies listed in the Yellow Pages and in Thomson Local directories will certainly be happy to hire out large pans, fish kettles and so on. They will also hire out equipment for keeping food warm but, in most instances, a bit of ingenuity and a careful choice of menu will solve the problems rather more cheaply.

Large salmon, for example, can be baked in the oven rather than poached in a large fish kettle (see pages 170–1) and preserving pans, Dutch ovens and large casseroles can be pressed into service for cooking vegetables. The chances are that a ring round relatives, friends and neighbours will probably provide all the pans you will need.

### KEEPING FOOD HOT

If you are planning to serve a lot of hot food you may need to think about your oven space on the day. Will you be able to cook and/or reheat sausage rolls, chicken drumsticks and pizza squares all within a relatively short time? Or would it be better to use the top of the stove for a couple of items, the small oven for a couple more, and to use the main oven to keep food hot before it goes out to the guests?

Other food can be prepared in advance and reheated in the microwave. However, if you do use a microwave oven for reheating, make sure that you leave the food in long enough to be heated right through to the centre.

## EQUIPMENT FOR THE RECEPTION

### TABLES AND CHAIRS

These are the first consideration and your requirements here will, of course, depend on the venue and the style of reception you have chosen. Most people can usually manage a large table or two for the buffet, but if you have a large number of guests you may need to hire trestle tables. These can also be useful as extra work surfaces. Catering equipment hire companies have these as well as all sizes of round tables for sit-down meals. Chairs too will come from the same source.

Tables and chairs are usually hired by the day, so you will need to time things fairly carefully if you are not to end up paying for two days.

### CROCKERY, CUTLERY AND GLASSES

You are very likely to need crockery, cutlery and glasses. If you are planning a canapés and drinks party you will only need to think about glasses – which can usually be borrowed from your wine merchant – and platters for the food. Trays and large dinner plates can be pressed into service here.

Finger buffets can also be managed with a napkin, but a fork buffet will need rather more in the way of equipment. One answer is to use paper plates and plastic cutlery, but this is not cheap to buy and you may decide that it is worth spending the extra money on hiring the real thing.

Most hire firms stock at least two styles of china, one very formal and the other rather less so. There may also be a choice of patterns. Similarly, there will be a choice of silver-plate or stainless-steel cutlery.

## COMPARE PRICES

Ring up a couple of your local firms and ask for their catalogues. You will then be able to compare terms and prices. Remember that most firms charge for delivery in addition to the individual hire charges. You will not notice this so much for large events, but it could substantially increase the cost of a small party.

When you come to order the equipment, make sure that you have worked things out in detail. Exactly which sizes of plate will you need? Do you want soup bowls with or without rims? Do you need condiment sets? What kind of glasses will be needed for the wine you are serving?

HERE'S A CHECKLIST FOR FORK BUFFET MENU 4 (SEE PAGES 165-6)
30 soup bowls
30 large dinner plates for the main course
30 dessert plates
2 large oval platters for the cheese logs
6 large bowls for the salads and fruit salad
6 large flat tart plates for the tart, flan and charlotte
30 soup spoons

30 large knives and forks
30 side knives
30 dessert spoons and forks
12 serving spoons
2 cake knives
3–4 cruet sets
3 bread-baskets
4 small plates for butter, etc.
30 coffee cups and saucers with matching milk jug and sugar bowl
40 glasses for reception drinks
40 glasses for wine with the meal
40 champagne flutes, if serving champagne

HERE'S A CHECKLIST FOR FINGER BUFFET MENU 1 (SEE PAGES 97–8)
2 white tablecloths for the drinks table and an occasional table
8 large oval platters for the food
8 large round platters for the food
6 small bowls for the dips
45 side or dessert plates for the food
45 small plates for the cake, if necessary
60 party goblets for the wine
45 champagne flutes, if serving champagne

**TIPS**

The platters should not be too large for a finger buffet. Once they are loaded with food they can be very heavy to carry around the assembled crowd.

If you do not have much help, you can often save on the washing up by sending the equipment back unwashed. However, most hire companies charge considerably more if they have to wash up their own dishes, glasses, crockery and cutlery.

## ELECTRICAL EQUIPMENT

If there are to be any speeches you will most probably need a microphone. This can be a good idea both for a large sit-down wedding breakfast and for a stand-up gathering in a large hall or in the garden. It will ensure that everyone hears the speeches and it also means that you can record them if you want to.

The only snag is the microphone – they can be a bit temperamental, so make sure someone who understands how it works is on hand to stop any high-pitched screeches or electrical crackling. Do make sure that those who are to speak also know how to use the microphone for there is nothing worse than watching and listening to someone fiddling with it before getting started on their speech.

Musical equipment is the other area of electrical equipment that might be worth thinking about. Music may be laid on as a background to the party or specifically for entertainment. If you plan to have dancing, it will, of course, be essential. Here again it is important to have someone around who really knows how the system works.

# CANAPÉS AND DRINKS RECEPTIONS

A canapés and drinks party can be a useful way of entertaining a large number of people. Less space is needed at this type of an event because the guests mostly stand up. It can also be fairly economical. The food is less expensive as it only consists of cocktail bites or canapés and, if you stick to wine, the drinks shouldn't be too expensive either. Indeed they may even cost less, as the party is unlikely to go on for quite so long.

A word of caution, though. It would be a mistake to think of a canapés and drinks party as a cheap option. It's true that you will probably be able to entertain more people for the same money, but you must still make sure that you put on a good spread. Cheap-skating at this type of party is just as bad as at a buffet or sit-down meal.

And another word of caution: the work involved is heavier than you might think. Canapés can be very time-consuming because they are fussy to make and to decorate. Hot items have to be cooked at the last minute and this means having someone in the kitchen throughout the event.

## THE PLAN

Start by looking at the catering master checklist (see pages 5–6). Work through it, adding the relevant sections to your own checklist.

Here are some extra points to consider as you go along.

## THE TIMING

This type of reception is ideal for events and weddings at odd times of the day. The bride and groom may be booked on a midday flight to the Far East or be off on an early evening train to Scotland and so will need to arrange the wedding ceremony at ten in the morning or two in the afternoon. Drinks and canapés are far more acceptable at these times of day than a sit-down meal.

## THE VENUE

Most venues work well for a canapés and drinks reception and quite often your own home is as good a place as any. By its nature, a stand-up event is rather cramped, but nobody gets left out in the cold.

If you are not sure just how many people you can cope with in your living room, calculate the standing space and allow about one square metre per person. Remember to allow for furniture you may be moving out and the drinks table you could be moving in.

A point to remember with family events like weddings and anniversaries is that there may well be elderly relatives about and they will almost certainly want to sit down after a while. So do have some chairs around, or set aside a room for those who want to sit.

## THE FOOD

There are no plates at a canapés and drinks party and so everything must be bite-sized or two bites at most. Quantities do not need to be very large; after all you are not providing a meal. Canapés are interesting accompaniments to the drinks.

The best way to plan quantities is to imagine a small plate and to think about how many canapés would fill it. This usually means eight to ten different items with perhaps a double portion of the more popular items, such as cocktail sausages. A mixture of hot and cold canapés is fine if you have help in the kitchen but in the summer, at least, it is not absolutely necessary.

It is easy to get carried away when deciding which canapés to serve. So check your menu and think about the time taken to prepare each item. Unless you are a really keen cook or have lots of helpers, it makes sense to mix some convenience items like frozen or ready-made vol-au-vents, frozen chicken nuggets and cooked smoked chicken cubes with more elaborate canapés such as Smoked Salmon Pinwheels, Oriental Bacon Rolls and Stuffed Dates.

It also makes sense to mix expensive with economical ingredients. If you plan to splash out on scampi, smoked trout or foie gras, you can balance them with plenty of cocktail sausages and cheese- or egg-based canapés.

One of the problems with cocktail food is that it is heavy on last-minute preparation. Canapé bases tend to go soggy quite quickly and hot food is always a last-minute job.

Advance preparation coupled with careful organisation on the day can help a lot. Vol-au-vent cases can be cooked and stored in airtight tins, choux pastry bouchés or puffs freeze well as do toppings such as chicken liver pâté and guacamole. Meatballs

33

and kofta, cheese straws, Chinese crab squares, Oriental bacon rolls and devils on horseback can all be frozen just prior to cooking or in their cooked state.

If you do decide to have some hot canapés, think about how they have to be cooked. It may be easier to use the oven to produce large quantities of cocktail sausages or vol-au-vents or to shallow-fry plenty of meatballs than it will be to deep-fry lots of scampi or goujons.

## COLD CANAPÉS
All kinds of ingredients can be pressed into service to make a really interesting array of canapés. Choose a variety of bases, toppings and garnishes and arrange together on trays. Keep square bases on one tray and round bases on another. Mini versions of popular finger food also make very good canapés.

## BASES
- Ciabatta, focaccia or brioche, toasted and cut into rounds or squares
- Fried bread cut into rounds or squares, crusts removed (see page 35)
- Rye bread or black pumpernickel cut into rounds or squares
- Cocktail oatcakes
- Small water biscuits
- Blinis
- Mini tartlet cases
- Choux pastry buns
- Mini Yorkshire puddings

> **TIP**
> Use fluted pastry cutters or, failing that, the rim of a small wine or sherry glass to cut the bread into rounds. Check that the glass is not chipped!

## SIMPLE TOPPINGS AND STUFFING FOR VEGETABLE CANAPÉS

- Cream cheese with garnish of keta or salmon caviar
- Smoked salmon or gravadlax
- Smoked Trout or Mackerel Pâté (page 52)
- Spiced Prawns (page 51)
- Slices of small-diameter salami or chorizo
- Mini rolls of Parma or Serrano ham (page 192)
- Creamed Brie cheese mixed with caraway seeds
- Mini mozzarella rounds with pesto sauce
- Chopped dates with cottage cheese and chervil (page 53)
- Chopped egg and asparagus (page 54)
- Guacamole (page 59)
- Chopped egg and watercress in mayonnaise
- Boursin, roulé or chèvre cheese
- Chicken Liver Pâté (page 49) or German liver sausage

## STUFFED VEGETABLES

- Cucumber rounds
- Celery sticks cut into short lengths
- Cherry tomatoes, hollowed out
- Button mushrooms, hollowed out
- Dates, stoned

## GARNISHES

- Tiny sprigs of fresh herbs
- Sprouted pea leaves
- Lumpfish or salmon caviar
- Capers or small caper berries
- Sliced gherkins or radishes
- A single red berry fruit: strawberry, raspberry or blackberry
- Piped mayonnaise rosette
- Pomegranate seeds

# CANAPÉ MENU 1

This is a relatively straightforward and inexpensive menu that is easy to prepare for large numbers.

## MENU

COLD

Mixed Liver Pâté (pages 49 and 50) canapés

Salmon Mousse canapés (page 55)

Smoked Turkey with Soured Cream and Cranberry Sauce on Blinis (page 57)

Aubergine Bruschetta (page 62)

Cocktail Kebabs (pages 68–9)

Goats' Cheese-stuffed Cherry Tomatoes (page 71)

HOT

Chicken Goujons with Spicy Tomato Sauce (page 82)

Cocktail Sausages with Mustard (page 96)

Spanish Tortilla Squares (page 138)

## PLAN

BUY IN READY-MADE

- Liver sausage and pâtés (optional)
- Smoked turkey, soured cream and cranberry sauce
- Cocktail kebab ingredients
- Blinis
- Cocktail sausages and mustard

## PREPARE IN ADVANCE

- Make liver pâtés if you prefer home-made, and refrigerate or freeze
- Make salmon mousse and refrigerate or freeze
- Make spicy sauce for goujons and refrigerate or freeze

## PREPARE EARLIER IN THE DAY AND COVER IN CLING FILM

- Thaw the liver pâtés, salmon mousse and spicy sauce, if in the freezer
- Make up cocktail kebabs
- Cook cocktail sausages to reheat just before serving
- Prepare chicken goujons
- Make the aubergine topping for the bruschetta
- Stuff cherry tomatoes with goats' cheese
- Make up liver pâté and salmon mousse canapés
- Prepare smoked turkey on blinis

## AT THE LAST MINUTE

- Toast ciabatta and make up aubergine bruschetta
- Make Spanish tortilla and cut into small squares
- Bake goujons and reheat spicy sauce
- Reheat sausages in microwave or oven

# CANAPÉ MENU 2

This is a little more expensive than Menu 1 and much more time-consuming to make. You will probably need extra help on the day.

## MENU

COLD
Hungarian Caviar Canapés (page 58)
Smoked Salmon Pinwheels (page 61)
Choux Puffs (page 136) with Guacamole (page 59)
Chicory spears with prawn cocktail

HOT
Scrambled Egg and Tarragon Vol-au-vents
Oriental Bacon Rolls (page 79)
Cocktail Koftas (page 84) with houmous
Chinese Crab Squares (page 77)
Italian Bruschetta with Herbs (page 63)

## PLAN

BUY IN READY-MADE
- Caviar, smoked salmon and fresh or canned crabmeat
- Prawn cocktail
- Vol-au-vents, fresh or frozen
- Houmous and guacamole

PREPARE IN ADVANCE
- Make choux puffs and store in an airtight tin or the freezer
- Make up cocktail kofta mixture and store in the fridge or freezer

## PREPARE EARLIER IN THE DAY AND COVER IN CLING FILM

- Thaw all frozen food
- Make Hungarian caviar mix for canapés and chill
- Make salmon pinwheels, slice, plate, decorate and chill
- Prepare bacon rolls and cocktail koftas; store in the fridge
- Make the topping for the crab squares and store in the fridge
- Spoon prawn cocktail onto chicory spears and chill
- Slice the Hungarian caviar mix for canapés, plate and decorate
- Prepare the tomato and herb topping for the bruschetta

## AT THE LAST MINUTE

- Fill choux puffs with guacamole
- Cook oriental bacon rolls and koftas
- Warm vol-au-vents in the oven
- Scramble the eggs and mix with tarragon and fill the vol-au-vents
- Fry Chinese crab squares
- Grill Italian bruschetta with herbs

# CANAPÉ MENU 3

This is a vegetarian menu but many of the items on it are just as popular with meat eaters. It is quite a quick and easy menu to prepare and serve.

## MENU

COLD

Mixed Vegetarian Canapés (page 35)
Savoury Cheese Truffles (page 92) and Stuffed Dates (page 53)
Nacho Chips with Guacamole (page 59)
Domino Tortilla Squares (page 138)
Chicory Spears with Orange Spiced Tabbouleh (page 128)
Parsley Stuffed Quail's Eggs

HOT

Blue-cheese Mini Tartlets (page 83)
Falafel with tahini dip
Hot Courgette Bites (page 76)

## PLAN

BUY IN READY-MADE

- Guacamole and nachos
- Falafel and tahini paste
- Ready-cooked and peeled quail's eggs

PREPARE IN ADVANCE

- Make blue-cheese tartlets and store in the freezer

PREPARE EARLIER IN THE DAY AND COVER IN CLING FILM

- Thaw the frozen tartlets
- Make savoury cheese truffles and stuffed dates; store in a cool place
- Make orange tabbouleh and use to top the chicory spears; chill; store in a cool place
- Cook the quail's eggs and stuff; do not chill
- Make mixed vegetarian canapés and store in a cool place
- Prepare and cook the domino tortilla squares; do not chill

AT THE LAST MINUTE

- Reheat the blue-cheese tartlets
- Heat the falafel and mix tahini paste with water to make a dip
- Fill the chicory spears with the orange tabbouleh
- Prepare and deep-fry the courgette bites
- Place guacamole in a bowl with the nacho chips

# CANAPÉ MENU 4

This is a canapé menu with an American theme that is fun to serve if there is any kind of US connection to the event. There are more hot canapés than cold in this menu, which is good for a winter party. It is not very difficult to prepare but there is quite a lot to do at the last minute, so make sure you have sufficient help in the kitchen. Try to keep all the items small and delicate.

## MENU

COLD

Cheese and Herb Lollipops (page 66)

Smoked Salmon, Dill and Horseradish Canapés on Rye (page 60)

Sherried Chicken Bites with Water Chestnuts (page 70)

HOT

Crunchy Potato Wedges (page 80) with Green Goddess Dip (pages 110–11)

Chilli con Carne Spoons (page 88) with Guacamole (page 59)

Mini Burgers Mixed (page 86) with cucumber relish

Cheese and Pecan 'Pizza' Squares (page 78)

Mini Hot-dog Sausages on Sticks with Mustard Dip (page 44)

## PLAN

BUY IN READY-MADE

- Mayonnaise
- Guacamole (optional)
- American cucumber relish

- Canned mini hot-dog sausages
- Canned water chestnuts

PREPARE IN ADVANCE
- Make chilli con carne and store in the freezer
- Prepare the sherried chicken and leave to marinate in the fridge
- Make guacamole, if not using ready-made, the day before, and store in the fridge

PREPARE EARLIER IN THE DAY AND COVER IN CLING FILM
- Make cheese and herb lollipops; keep cool in the fridge
- Prepare the sherried chicken bites with water chestnuts; keep cool in the fridge
- Thaw chilli con carne
- Make smoked salmon, dill and horseradish canapés; keep cool in the fridge
- Prepare the mixes for the mini burgers and store in the fridge
- Prepare a mustard dip for the hot-dog sausages by mixing half and half mustard and mayonnaise
- Make green goddess dip and store in the fridge

AT THE LAST MINUTE
- Prepare and roast the crunchy potato wedges
- Cook burgers and display
- Cook cheese and pecan pizza squares
- Heat mini hot-dog sausages in hot water
- Reheat chilli con carne, arrange in Chinese china/porcelain soup spoons and garnish

# CANAPÉ MENU 5

This is a special-occasion fish and vegetarian menu but many of the items on it are just as popular with meat eaters. There is a fair amount of preparation to do on the day for this menu as well as a good deal of last-minute cooking, so keep the numbers down or organise plenty of helpers in the kitchen.

## MENU

COLD
Artichoke Hearts with Potted Shrimps (page 65)
Stuffed Chicory Spears with Egg and Anchovies (page 72)
Crunchy Smoked Salmon and Vegetable Bites (page 56)
Crab Mayonnaise in Wafer Tartlets (page 64)

HOT
Tapenade Catherine Wheels (page 91)
Deep-fried Smoked Trout Balls with Tartare Sauce (page 90)
Creamy Prawn Vol-au-vents (page 75)
Seared Scallops on Fried Croutes with Ginger (page 81)

## PLAN

BUY IN READY-MADE
- Fresh or frozen vol-au-vents
- Japanese sliced ginger
- Canned prepared artichoke hearts
- Wafer tartlets
- Tartare sauce

PREPARE IN ADVANCE
- Prepare the Catherine wheels and store uncooked in the freezer

PREPARE EARLIER IN THE DAY AND COVER IN CLING FILM
- Thaw Catherine wheels
- Prepare the artichokes stuffed with potted shrimps; store in the fridge
- Prepare stuffed chicory spears with egg and anchovies; store in a cool place
- Prepare the crunchy smoked salmon bites; store in a cool place
- Prepare the crab mayonnaise and store in the fridge
- Prepare the fried croutes for the scallops and keep on one side
- Make the prawn filling for the vol-au-vents

AT THE LAST-MINUTE
- Fill the crab-mayonnaise tartlets
- Bake the Catherine wheels
- Deep-fry the trout balls
- Heat the prawn filling for the vol-au-vents
- Fill the prawn vol-au-vents
- Fry the scallops and arrange on the fried-bread croutes

# THE DRINKS

The easiest drink to serve at a canapés and drinks party is champagne or a good sparkling wine (see page 18). Alternatively, you could offer a choice of red and white wine with a glass of champagne for the toasts, if any.

Choose light wines. You will not be serving a large meal and when wine is drunk on its own or with canapés it should not be too assertive. Talk to your supplier and when you have chosen the wine, try a bottle of each at home one evening.

# THE EQUIPMENT

Equipment is not really a problem with this type of food. You may want to borrow a bit of freezer space or perhaps a large electric deep-fat fryer and you will need plenty of baking trays for the oven or microwave cooker, but not masses of crockery and cutlery. What you will need are plenty of trays on which to arrange the food and a large number of glasses.

Allow at least 50 per cent more glasses than guests, as people tend to lose track of their glasses.

You will also need cocktail sticks, paper napkins, ashtrays, corkscrews, bottle openers and somewhere to put the ice.

# STAFF AND HELPERS

The cold food can be left on a buffet table or be scattered around the room, but the hot food really does need to be handed round and the drinks need to be served. You will need at least one helper for every fifteen people and one helper to ten guests for hot food. Remember there may be a change of drinks for the toasts and, if having, there is also the cake to distribute. The best method is to ask half the staff to deal with drinks and the other half to deal with the food.

The amount of help you need in the kitchen will depend upon how much needs to be finished off at the last minute and how much hot food you are having.

# THE RECIPES

# CHICKEN LIVER PÂTÉ

You can, of course, easily buy in ready-made chicken liver pâté but home-made is much nicer – and cheaper! Use this chicken liver pâté to stuff button mushrooms or cherry tomatoes or to fill small cocktail tartlets or choux balls. It also makes an excellent canapé topping. Choose slices of toasted brioche for a really sumptuous effect.

**Makes about 675g**

**350g butter**
**2 small onions, finely chopped**
**450g chicken livers**
**2 tbsp Southern Comfort, brandy or sherry**
**5–6 drops Tabasco pepper sauce**
**½ tsp dried thyme**
**Salt and freshly ground black pepper**
**Sage leaves, capers or slices of small gherkins, for decoration**

1. Melt 100g of the butter and fry the onions for 2–3 minutes. Add the chicken livers and cook for a further 3–4 minutes, stirring all the time. Add the rest of the butter and all the remaining ingredients. Stir until the butter melts.
2. Chop the mixture in a food processor or purée in a blender. Leave to cool.
3. Spread on canapés and decorate with sage leaves, capers or slices of small gherkins.

# DANISH LIVER PÂTÉ

This economical pâté can be sliced and served on a buffet or as a starter at a sit-down meal. It can also be thinly sliced or roughly chopped and used as an excellent topping for canapés of various kinds. Garnish with crisply fried onions or pickled red cabbage.

**Makes 8 slices (or sufficient for 30 canapés)**

300g pig's liver
225g streaky bacon
1 onion, finely chopped
1 tbsp chopped anchovies
½ tsp allspice
Salt and freshly ground black pepper
25g butter
25g plain flour
300ml milk
1 egg, beaten

1. Mince the liver, bacon and onion twice or blend in a food processor. Add chopped anchovies and the allspice and seasoning. Mix well together and keep on one side.
2. Preheat the oven to 160°C/325°F/Gas 3.
3. Melt the butter in a pan and stir in the flour. Gradually add the milk, stirring all the time, and bring to the boil. Remove the pan from the heat and beat in the liver mixture and the egg.
4. Spoon into a 450g loaf tin and cover with foil. Bake in a large roasting tin filled with 2cm hot water for 1–1½ hours. The pâté is cooked when a skewer inserted into the centre comes out clean. Cool with a heavy weight on the top of the pâté.
5. Turn out and slice.

# SPICED PRAWNS

Use as a canapé topping or to fill small vol-au-vents. These spicy prawns also taste good on spears of Belgium endive.

**Makes 350g**

225g peeled prawns, chopped
10 pimento-stuffed olives, finely chopped
1 bunch spring onions, finely chopped
50g flaked almonds, toasted
Juice of ½ lemon
1 tsp extra virgin olive oil
1 tsp tomato purée
Dash of Worcestershire sauce
Salt and pepper

1. Place all the ingredients in a basin and mix well together. Chill until required.

# SMOKED TROUT OR MACKEREL PÂTÉ

Use as a canapé topping for little rounds of fried bread or for brown bread pinwheels.

**Makes sufficient for 30 canapés**

**1kg smoked trout or mackerel fillets**
**200g butter, softened**
**2 tbsp olive oil**
**4 tbsp horseradish cream**
**150g fromage frais or quark**
**Juice of 2 large lemons**
**Salt and freshly ground black pepper**

1. Remove any bones from the smoked fish and mince very finely.
2. Place the butter and oil in a mixing bowl and cream together until well blended. Gradually beat in the minced smoked fish and then the horseradish cream, fromage frais or quark and lemon juice.
3. Season to taste.

# CHOPPED DATES WITH COTTAGE CHEESE AND CHERVIL

Use for rye bread canapés or spoon small amounts onto small spears of Belgian endive.

**Makes about 40**

**300g soft cottage cheese**
**200g stoned dates, finely chopped**
**Small bunch fresh chervil**
**Salt and freshly ground black pepper**
**100g pine nuts, toasted**

1. Mix all the ingredients, except the pine nuts, together in a bowl.
2. Shape with a teaspoon into small balls and coat with toasted pine nuts.

# STUFFED DATES

Here's an idea for those with a sweet tooth.

**Makes 50**

**50 fresh dates**
**225g cream cheese**
**75g ground almonds**
**3 tbsp Amaretto**

1. Slit the dates and remove the stones.
2. Mix all the remaining ingredients together and stuff into the dates.

# CHOPPED EGG AND ASPARAGUS

This mixture makes a good topping for fried bread canapés or it can be used in mini tartlets or vol-au-vents. You can easily make a similar topping using a bunch of watercress instead of asparagus.

**Makes sufficient for 50 canapés (or 35 mini tartlets)**

**10 eggs**
**20 spears asparagus, chopped**
**4 tbsp mayonnaise**
**Salt and freshly ground black pepper**

1.  Hard-boil the eggs, shell and lightly chop with a knife. Add the mayonnaise and seasoning to taste and mash with a fork.
2.  Fold in the asparagus.

# ECONOMICAL SALMON MOUSSE

This recipe goes back to my childhood when fresh salmon was exceedingly expensive. Even today canned salmon is a cheaper option for large-scale catering and the results from this very economical recipe are excellent.

**Makes about 750g**

**2 x 170g tins skinned and boned salmon**
**About 400ml milk**
**50g butter**
**50g plain flour**
**Salt and freshly ground black pepper**
**1 egg, beaten**
**Slivers of sliced lemon or sprigs of chervil or parsley, for**
  **decoration**

1. Drain any liquid from the salmon and make up to 450ml with milk.
2. Melt the butter in a pan, add the flour, stir and add the milk mixture. Bring the mixture to the boil, whisking all the time with a wire whisk or beating with a wooden spoon. Cook the sauce for 3 minutes to give a medium consistency.
3. Flake the salmon and mash with a fork. Add to the sauce and season to taste. Remove from the heat and beat in the egg.
4. Spoon the mixture into two small lightly greased ½ litre (450g) pudding basins. Cover with foil held in place with a rubber band and place in a large pan with 3–5cm water in the base. Bring the water to the boil. Reduce the heat and simmer for 45 minutes.
5. Leave to cool in the basins. Spread on canapés and decorate with slivers of sliced lemon or sprigs of chervil or parsley. Turn out if serving as a starter and cut into wedges.

# CRUNCHY SMOKED SALMON AND VEGETABLE BITES

This mixture makes an excellent topping for fried-bread croutes, blinis or toasted rye bread. It also makes a good filling for a shortcrust pastry tart. Blind bake the tart, cool and fill with the mixture.

**Makes 24 bites (or sufficient to fill an 18cm tart)**

75g smoked salmon
100g cream cheese
4 tbsp finely chopped red pepper
1 tbsp finely chopped celery
1 tbsp finely chopped spring onion
Salt and freshly ground black pepper
A little lemon juice

1. Mix all the ingredients together, adding sufficient lemon juice to give the mix a creamy spreading consistency.
2. Spread onto your chosen base.

# SMOKED TURKEY WITH SOURED CREAM AND CRANBERRY SAUCE ON BLINIS

If you cannot find blinis, simply use rye bread or fried-bread bases.

**Makes 50**

50 blinis
2 x 450g jars cranberry sauce
650g smoked turkey, sliced and cut into small pieces
250ml soured cream
Salt and freshly ground black pepper
Bunch fresh dill or chervil, for decoration

1. Spread the blinis with cranberry sauce.
2. Arrange small slices of smoked turkey on top and add a blob of soured cream.
3. Season to taste and decorate with fresh dill or chervil.

# HUNGARIAN CAVIAR CANAPÉS

Serve this delicious mixture on circles of German pumpernickel or, if preferred, a lighter rye bread.

**Makes 36**

110g tin small sardines in brine or oil, drained
1 very small onion, grated
175g butter, softened
1 x 100g jar black lumpfish caviar
75g cream cheese
1 x 100g jar red lumpfish caviar
2–3 baby cucumbers, cut into 18 x 5mm thick slices
6 small tomatoes, cut into 18 slices
Slices of rye bread, cut into rounds
Sprigs of parsley, for decoration

1. Rub the sardines through a sieve and mix with half the grated onion and half the butter. Stir in the black caviar.
2. Shape in foil into a long roll the same diameter as the cucumbers and refrigerate.
3. Mix the cream cheese with the remaining onion and butter and red caviar.
4. Shape as above and refrigerate.
5. When the black and red caviar rolls have set (about 1½–2 hours), cut each roll into 18 thick slices. Top the cucumber with rounds of red caviar mix, and the tomatoes with rounds of black caviar mix.
6. Butter the rounds of rye bread and top with the cucumber and tomato slices. Decorate with sprigs of parsley and serve.

# GUACAMOLE

You can easily buy ready-made guacamole but the home-made version is much cheaper and can taste better. Use as a canapé topping or as a dip with nachos or vegetable crudités.

**Makes 350g**

**2 tbsp lemon juice**
**2 ripe tomatoes, finely chopped**
**2 tbsp finely chopped onion**
**6 sprigs coriander, finely chopped**
**Salt and freshly ground black pepper**
**2 ripe avocados**

1. Mix together all the ingredients, except the avocados, and chill until required.
2. Peel and stone the avocados and mash the flesh with a fork, or purée in a blender.
3. Stir into the tomato and onion mixture.

# SMOKED SALMON, DILL AND HORSERADISH CANAPÉS ON RYE

German pumpernickel bread makes a good base for these canapés, but any kind of rye bread will do. They are very popular, so make sufficient for at least two canapés per person.

**Makes 64**

16 slices pumpernickel
3 tbsp horseradish cream
I bunch dill, finely chopped
600g smoked salmon
2 lemons, sliced very thinly
1 pickled cucumber, sliced very thinly
Lemon or cucumber slices, for decoration
Freshly ground black pepper

1. Spread the slices of pumpernickel with the horseradish cream and sprinkle with chopped dill (reserve a little for the garnish).
2. Place two layers of smoked salmon, cut to size, on top. Cut each slice into four canapés.
3. Decorate with a slice of lemon or a slice of cucumber and a little more dill. Finish with plenty of freshly ground black pepper.

# PINWHEELS

Pinwheels are made by removing the crusts from brown or white sliced bread. The bread is then spread with a suitable creamy filling or with butter and sliced meat or fish. To achieve a really elegant effect, roll each slice of bread with a rolling pin before adding the filling.

**Slices of white or brown bread, crusts removed**

*Fillings*
**Liver sausage or pâté (pages 49, 50 and 52)**
**Salmon Mousse (page 55)**
**Cream cheese mixed with fresh herbs, chopped smoked salmon or toasted sesame seeds**
**Sliced tongue**
**Sliced smoked ham or loin of pork**
**Sliced smoked salmon or trout**

*Garnish*
**Box of cress**

1. Spread or place the filling on the rolled bread slices. Roll the filled bread into small Swiss rolls and slice.
2. Once sliced, arrange on a serving platter and keep fresh by wrapping the platter in cling film.
3. Just before serving, garnish with freshly cut cress from the box.

**TIP**
Pinwheels can be packed into rigid polythene boxes before they are sliced, and deep-frozen. Allow plenty of time on the day to thaw them out. This means at least 2–3 hours, or more, depending on the size of the box.

# AUBERGINE BRUSCHETTA

This is another really versatile item, which can be cut into various sizes to suit the format of the meal.

**Makes 36–48**

3 medium aubergines
4 spring onions, seeded and finely chopped
1 small red pepper, seeded and finely chopped
Salt and freshly ground black pepper
I large ciabatta loaf, sliced
2 cloves garlic, peeled and cut in half
Extra virgin olive oil

1. Bake the aubergines at 190°C/375°F/Gas 5 for about 30 minutes until tender.
2. Split open with a knife and scrape out all the flesh, discarding the skin. Mash with a fork and mix with the spring onions, pepper and seasoning.
3. Rub the slices of bread all over with the cut side of the garlic and place on a lined baking tray. Drizzle with plenty of extra virgin olive oil and toast under the grill, turning the slices as they brown.
4. Spread the aubergine mixture over the toasted ciabatta and cut into three or four thick slices, depending on the type of buffet. Serve at once.

# ITALIAN BRUSCHETTA WITH HERBS

You can use virtually any fresh herb in this bruschetta recipe. Basil is the classic choice, but parsley, chervil and dill are all good choices. For something really punchy go for fresh coriander or mint.

**Makes 12**

**Small ciabatta loaf, cut in half lengthways into two flat slices**
**Olive oil**
**1 tbsp tapenade, anchoïade or olive paste**

*Tomato and herb topping*
**2–3 cloves garlic, peeled and finely chopped**
**4–5 tbsp olive oil**
**2 tomatoes, chopped**
**1 tbsp fresh herbs – basil, parsley or tarragon**
**Salt and freshly ground black pepper**

*Garnish*
**Stuffed green olives, sliced**
**Sprigs of herbs**

1. Start by making the tomato and herb topping. Fry the garlic in oil until well browned, taking care not to burn. Leave to cool in a bowl.
2. Add the tomatoes, herbs and seasoning to the bowl and leave to stand until required.
3. Brush the ciabatta slices with a little olive oil and toast under the grill. Spread with tapenade or olive paste and pile the tomato mixture on top.
4. Just before serving, return to the grill for 3–4 minutes.
5. To serve, cut each ciabatta slice into six small pieces. Arrange on serving plates and garnish each one with a slice of olive and a tiny sprig of matching herbs to those used in the mix.

# CRAB MAYONNAISE
# IN WAFER TARTLETS

Tiny wafer tartlets are now on sale in many supermarkets. Do not fill them until the last minute as they have a tendency to go soggy. This mixture can also be used on canapé bases and in vol-au-vent cases.

**Makes 24**

**2 x 200g tins white crab meat**
**2 tbsp mayonnaise**
**Salt and freshly ground black pepper**
**24 wafer tartlets**

1. Pick over the crab meat to remove any bits of shell which might have been left in.
2. Mix with the mayonnaise and season to taste.
3. Chill and use to fill the tartlets just before serving.

# ARTICHOKE HEARTS WITH POTTED SHRIMPS

Fresh artichokes are very fiddly to prepare and it is much easier to use canned artichokes. The best ones to choose are the ones with all the leaves removed, packed in stacks in the can. If you cannot find these, use the small artichoke hearts that still have some small leaves attached. Cut in half and cut a sliver off the base so that they will stay flat on the serving plate.

**Makes 24**

24 artichoke hearts (about 6 cans)
6 cartons potted shrimps in butter
2 tbsp lemon juice
Salt and freshly ground black pepper
Small sprigs chervil, parsley or dill, for garnish

1.  Drain the artichoke hearts well and arrange on a large platter.
2.  Empty the contents of the cartons of potted shrimps into a bowl and add the lemon juice, salt and pepper. Mix together gently, breaking up any larger lumps of butter.
3.  Spoon a little of the potted shrimps onto each artichoke heart and garnish with your chosen herb.

# CHEESE AND HERB LOLLIPOPS

These are mini versions of the large flavoured cheese balls with crudités that I have often enjoyed with an apéritif instead of a first course at American dinner parties. There are numerous variations on the theme, made with different herbs and coatings. Here are three examples to mix on the serving plate. For an attractive presentation, serve on cocktail sticks stuck into half a large melon.

**Each recipe makes about 40**

## DATE AND BASIL

**300g soft cheese such as Philadelphia**
**200g stoned dates, finely chopped**
**1 bunch fresh basil, around 6–7 sprigs**
**Salt and freshly ground black pepper**
**200g pine nuts, toasted**

1. Mix all the ingredients, except the pine nuts, together in a bowl.
2. Shape with a teaspoon into small balls and coat with toasted pine nuts.

## GINGER AND SPRING ONION

**200g soft cheese such as Philadelphia**
**1 bunch spring onions, finely chopped**
**4cm fresh root ginger, peeled and grated**
**50g ground almonds**
**Freshly ground black pepper**
**150g sesame seeds, toasted**

1. Mix all the ingredients, except the sesame seeds, together in a bowl.
2. Shape with a teaspoon into small balls and coat with toasted sesame seeds.

## TUNA AND WALNUT

**2 x 114g tins tuna, drained and mashed**
**200g soft cheese such as Philadelphia**
**35g walnuts, finely chopped**
**¼ small onion, finely chopped**
**Salt and freshly ground black pepper**
**5–6 tbsp freshly chopped parsley**

1. Mash the tuna with a fork and mix with all the remaining ingredients except the parsley.
2. Shape with a teaspoon into small balls and coat with the chopped parsley.

# COCKTAIL KEBABS ON A STICK

An interesting variety of small bites gathered together on cocktail sticks looks as attractive as it tastes. For an old-fashioned but effective presentation, plunge the end of each cocktail stick into a large melon and display as the centrepiece of a canapé buffet. Or, if the canapés are to be handed round, use small half melons or large grapefruit halves as the base.

All kinds of cubed or sliced fruit, vegetables, meats and cheese can be pressed into service on this versatile theme. For more ideas for more substantial cold kebabs, see Salad Kebabs, page 127.

Here are some ideas for combinations to try:

Halved strawberries
Cubes of Brie
Chunks of baby corn

Tiny rolls of Serrano ham
Basil leaves
Cubes of melon

Halved cherry tomatoes
Cubes of smoked turkey
Diced kiwifruit

Diced pears
Cubes of Stilton cheese
Cherry tomato halves

Smoked ham cubes
Tinned peach cubes
Diced cucumber

Salami cubes
Cocktail gherkins
Cubes of beetroot

**TIP**

If you are serving canapés on cocktail sticks remember to provide plenty of ashtrays for people to dump their sticks. The waitress always seems to have just moved away as you swallow the item, and anyway, lots of discarded sticks on the serving tray doesn't look good.

# SHERRIED CHICKEN BITES
# WITH WATER CHESTNUTS

This recipe must be made well in advance. In fact, the longer the chicken marinates the better it will taste. Choose dry oloroso sherry for a really definite taste, but if you are not sure go for fino sherry. If you cannot find water chestnuts, try looking in oriental stores.

**Makes about 35**

**8 chicken breast fillets**
**Dry fino or dry oloroso sherry**
**3 x 325g tins water chestnuts**
**Slivers of Japanese white ginger**
**Small cocktail sticks**
**Spring onion flowers, for garnish – made by splitting the**
  **spring onion lengthways, two or three times, down to the**
  **bulb, and opening out in water**

1. Wrap the chicken breasts in kitchen foil and bake at 190°C/375°F/Gas 5 for about 45 minutes until they are cooked through.
2. Remove from the foil and arrange in a large plastic container and completely cover with sherry. Place some crumpled foil on the top of the chicken to keep it submerged in the sherry, replace the lid and place in the fridge. Leave for 3–4 days to marinate.
3. To serve, cut the chicken into cubes and thread on to cocktail sticks interspersed with water chestnuts and slivers of Japanese white ginger. Arrange on a serving plate and garnish with spring onion flowers.

# GOATS' CHEESE STUFFED CHERRY TOMATOES

Choose small cherry tomatoes to use as canapés and stuff with a fresh, soft rindless goats' cheese such as Chavroux.

**Makes 50**

**25 cherry tomatoes**
**300g soft goats' cheese**

*Garnish*
**2–3 tbsp toasted pine nuts**
**5–6 sprigs fresh dill, broken into small pieces**
**Freshly ground black pepper**

1. Cut the tomatoes in half across the middle and scoop out the hard centres and seeds, and discard.
2. Place small teaspoonfuls of the goats' cheese into each tomato half. Top with 3–4 pine nuts and a small piece of dill. Sprinkle with freshly ground black pepper.

# STUFFED CHICORY SPEARS WITH EGG AND ANCHOVIES

Choose small heads of chicory so that the spears are not too large for a canapé buffet. Keep the outside leaves for a salad another day.

**Makes 50**

10 eggs, hard-boiled
4 tbsp mayonnaise
20 small cherry tomatoes, finely chopped
2 tbsp freshly chopped dill
Salt to taste
12 heads chicory
50 anchovy fillets
Freshly ground black pepper

1. Peel and roughly chop the eggs. Add the mayonnaise and mash with a fork. Stir in the tomatoes, dill and salt to taste and keep on one side.
2. Peel off 50 spears from the chicory and arrange in circles on large trays with the spears pointing out. Spoon the egg and tomato mixture down the centre of each and top with an anchovy fillet.
3. Serve sprinkled with freshly ground black pepper.

# PORCINI CROSTINI TOPPING

This makes a very rich topping that can be used to make canapés or finger food for a buffet; fried-bread squares are particularly good here. Alternatively, serve on a bed of rocket with strips of roasted red peppers and toasted ciabatta bread. This makes an excellent first course. Save the liquor in which the porcini have been reconstituted and use to flavour soups or casserole stocks.

**Makes 750g**

**25g dried porcini, soaked in boiling water for 1 hour**
**6 tbsp olive oil**
**2 onions, finely chopped**
**2 cloves garlic, peeled and crushed**
**350g open mushrooms, very finely chopped**
**4 tbsp dry white wine**
**6 tbsp freshly chopped parsley**
**1 tbsp ground almonds**
**1 tbsp dried oregano**
**Pinch of dried thyme**
**Salt and freshly ground black pepper**

1. Finely chop the porcini and keep on one side.
2. Heat the oil and fry the onion and garlic until transparent. Add the mushrooms and fry for a further 2–3 minutes.
3. Add all the remaining ingredients – including the porcini and a little of its soaking juices – and simmer for half an hour until all the juices have been used up and the mixture is thick. Leave to cool.
4. Chill slightly before serving in your chosen manner.

# VOL-AU-VENT FILLINGS

You can buy very good ready-made fresh or frozen vol-au-vent cases in various sizes so they can form part of a canapé buffet or finger buffet. They will just need to be heated in the oven before filling.

**Makes sufficient for 35 finger buffet vol-au-vents
and about 50 canapé vol-au-vents**

## CHICKEN AND MUSHROOM FILLING

**200g cooked chicken meat**
**25g butter**
**2 tbsp olive oil**
**200g button mushrooms, finely chopped**

*White sauce*
**100ml butter**
**150g plain flour**
**900ml milk**
**100ml white wine**
**Salt and freshly ground black pepper**

1. Cut the chicken into small pieces; the smaller the vol-au-vent cases, the smaller the chicken pieces need to be.
2. Heat the butter and oil in a frying pan, add the mushrooms and fry gently for about 5–6 minutes until they soften. Stir in the chicken pieces and keep on one side while you make the white sauce.
3. Place the butter in a pan over a medium heat and allow to melt. Stir in the flour and add the milk and wine. Whisk the

mixture on the heat until it thickens. Bring to the boil, lower the heat and simmer for 3 minutes. If you are making the sauce in advance, cover with cling film and leave until required. To use, add a little more milk and carefully bring back to the boil.

4. Stir in the mushroom and chicken mixture and season to taste.
5. Fill the heated vol-au-vent cases with the mixture and serve at once.

## CREAMY PRAWN FILLING

**250g small peeled prawns**

*White sauce*
**100ml butter**
**150g plain flour**
**800ml milk**
**100ml double cream**
**100ml white wine**
**Salt and freshly ground black pepper**

1. Start by making the white sauce. Place the butter in a pan over a medium heat and allow to melt. Stir in the flour and add the milk, cream and wine. Whisk the mixture on the heat until it thickens. Bring to the boil, lower the heat and simmer for 3 minutes.
2. If you are making the sauce in advance, cover with cling film and leave until required. To use, add a little more milk and carefully bring back to the boil.
3. Stir in the prawns and season to taste.
4. Fill the heated vol-au-vent cases with the mixture and serve at once.

# COURGETTE BITES

You can make similar bites with cooked aubergines or peppers. If it is a large event, make batches of all three and serve together.

**Makes 36**

**3–4 courgettes, depending on size**
**250g grated Cheddar cheese**
**1 tsp dried oregano**
**Salt and freshly ground black pepper**
**Plain flour (optional)**
**8 large slices bread, buttered**
**4 eggs, beaten**
**Cooking oil, for frying**

1. Steam the courgettes whole until cooked through. Mash with a fork.
2. Allow the mixture to cool and then mix with the grated cheese, oregano, salt and pepper. If the mixture is a bit wet, add a little plain flour.
3. Spread the mixture onto four slices of bread and top with the remaining four slices.
4. Cut each sandwich into 9 squares. Dip in beaten egg and fry quickly on both sides in very hot cooking oil. Serve at once.

**TIP**
Remember to allow a cooling-off period for deep-fried or oven-cooked items, otherwise your guests will easily burn their fingers as well as their tongues.

# CHINESE CRAB SQUARES

A good variation on this theme can be made with finely chopped prawns.

**Makes 36**

350g white crab meat
8 spring onions, very finely chopped
1 tsp freshly grated root ginger
1 egg, beaten
1 tbsp cornflour
Salt and freshly ground black pepper
6 slices white bread, crusts removed
3 tbsp sesame seeds
Cooking oil, for frying

1. Mix the crab meat with the spring onions, ginger, egg, cornflour and seasoning.
2. Spread this mixture over the slices of bread and sprinkle with sesame seeds. Press the seeds on well using the flat blade of a knife. Cut each slice into 4 squares.
3. Heat about 1cm cooking oil in a large frying pan and fry the slices of toast, a few at a time, first on the bread side and then on the crab side, for 45–60 seconds each side. The toast should be golden all over.
4. Serve at once.

# CHEESE AND PECAN 'PIZZA' SQUARES

I was tempted to use 'American cheese' for this recipe for its lovely bright yellow colour. However, this is not really cheese but a processed product which does not have the kind of strong flavour needed here. Instead, I chose Cheddar made with annatto, the dye from a tropical fruit, which also has a bright orange yellow colour. If you have access to an American grocer, try Monterey Jack.

**Makes 36**

**6 slices thickly sliced wholemeal (bread)**
**6 tbsp olive oil**
**300g orange/yellow Cheddar cheese, grated**
**75g pecan nuts, chopped**
**2 tbsp American sweet mustard**
**1½ tbsp A1 or Worcestershire sauce**
**Freshly ground black pepper**

1. Allowing 1 tablespoon olive oil for each slice, fry the bread on each side in hot oil until well browned. Drain on kitchen paper.
2. Mix all the remaining ingredients in a bowl. Spread this mixture over the slices of fried bread, making sure that the topping goes right up to the edges.
3. Place under a hot grill for 2 minutes until the mixture just starts to bubble. Remove from the heat and cut each slice into six pieces.
4. Arrange on a serving plate. Try serving with the mini hot dog sausages on sticks and the mustard dip (page 44).

# ORIENTAL BACON ROLLS

This is a variation on devils on horseback where chicken livers rather than prunes are wrapped in streaky bacon and fried or cooked under the grill. If the party is quite a large one, add prunes wrapped in bacon as another option.

**Makes 50**

4 chicken breast fillets, skinned
25 rashers streaky bacon, cut in two vertically
12 chicken livers, cut in half
2 tbsp olive oil

*Marinade*
2 tbsp extra virgin olive oil
6 tbsp soy sauce
2 tbsp sherry
Juice and grated rind of 1 orange
Pinch ground cloves and cinnamon or Chinese five spice powder
Salt and freshly ground black pepper

1. Cut each chicken breast into 6–7 pieces and wrap a rasher of bacon round each one. Secure with a cocktail stick.
2. Mix the marinade ingredients together and pour over the chicken rolls. Leave to stand until the start of the event.
3. Wrap the remaining bacon round each piece of chicken liver and secure in the same way.
4. Ten minutes before serving, place the chicken and bacon rolls and their marinade in a saucepan and bring to the boil. Reduce the heat and simmer for 8 minutes.
5. Fry the chicken liver and bacon rolls in olive oil until well browned, turning from time to time.

# CRUNCHY POTATO WEDGES WITH GREEN GODDESS DIP

You will need to make plenty of these crunchy potato wedges, they simply disappear off the plate. See pages 110–11 for the recipe for Green Goddess Dip.

**Serves about 50**

**3kg small floury potatoes, skin on**
**200ml olive oil**
**4 cloves garlic, peeled and crushed**
**1 tbsp mixed dried herbs**
**1 tsp smoked or plain paprika pepper**
**Coarse sea salt, to serve**

1. Preheat the oven to 200°C/400°F/Gas 6.
2. Slice the potatoes in half lengthways and cut each half into four wedges. Place in a large bowl.
3. Mix all the remaining ingredients together in a jug and pour over the potato wedges. Toss together until the wedges are well coated with the flavoured oil.
4. You will probably need to use two shelves in the oven or to cook the wedges in batches. Arrange as many, skin side down, as you can get on a baking tray. Bake in the oven for about 40 minutes until well browned and crispy at the edges.
5. Transfer to a serving platter and sprinkle with sea salt. Serve with Green Goddess Dip.

# SEARED SCALLOPS ON FRIED CROUTES WITH GINGER

The Japanese ginger used in this recipe is the kind of ginger that is served with sushi in Japanese restaurants; it is spicy but not too hot. Shape the small slices into curls or rolls to give some height to the canapés.

**Makes 36**

**9 slices thick white bread**
**Cooking oil, for deep-frying**
**36 small scallops, or 18 larger scallops sliced in half**
**2 tbsp olive oil**
**25g butter**
**1 jar Japanese white sliced ginger**
**Sprouted alfalfa**

1.  Start by preparing the fried croutes. Cut four small rounds out of each slice of bread and deep-fry in cooking oil until golden and crisp. Drain on kitchen paper.
2.  Place the olive oil and butter in a heavy-based frying pan and fry the scallops quickly on each side until lightly golden in colour and cooked through.
3.  Place one scallop on each fried croute and top with a piece of sliced ginger.
4.  Arrange the croutes on a bed of alfalfa.

# CHICKEN GOUJONS
# WITH SPICY TOMATO SAUCE

The sauce can be made in advance and frozen. It is a good idea to advise your guests that peanuts have been used in this recipe.

**Serves approx. 24**

**6 medium chicken breast fillets, skinned**
**Plain flour**
**Salt and freshly ground black pepper**
**6 tbsp wholenut peanut butter**
**3 eggs, beaten**

*Sauce*
**2 green chilli peppers, seeded and chopped**
**3 cloves garlic, peeled and chopped**
**2 tbsp olive oil**
**2 x 400g tins tomatoes**
**1 tsp sugar**
**Salt and freshly ground black pepper**

1. Preheat the oven to 190°C/375°F/Gas 5.
2. Cut the chicken into bite-sized pieces and toss in seasoned flour.
3. Beat the peanut butter and eggs together to form a thick purée. Dip the chicken pieces in this mixture. Shake well and place on oiled foil on a baking tray
4. Bake for 15–20 minutes. The coating should be quite crisp and brown.
5. To prepare the sauce, gently fry the green chilli and garlic in the olive oil for 2–3 minutes. Add the contents of the tins of tomatoes and bring to the boil. Stir in the sugar and seasoning, cover and simmer for 20 minutes.
6. Sieve or process the sauce in a blender. Reheat and serve with the baked goujons.

# BLUE-CHEESE MINI TARTLETS

This French classic is usually made with Roquefort but you could use Stilton or any good creamy blue cheese.

**Makes 50**

**500g puff pastry**
**Plain flour, for rolling out**
**100g walnuts, chopped**
**300g blue cheese**
**4 eggs**
**120ml double cream**

1. Preheat the oven to 190°C/375°F/Gas 5.
2. Roll out the pastry on a floured surface/board and use pastry cutter or a glass of the right size to cut out rounds. Use to line mini tartlet tins.
3. Mix together all the remaining ingredients and spoon into the prepared pastry cases. Bake for about 10–12 minutes. Leave to cool a little and serve warm.

# COCKTAIL KOFTAS

These spicy meatballs make delicious nibbles to serve on sticks. Serve on a bed of cress or alfalfa sprouts with a spicy dip (see opposite).

**Makes 50**

8 tbsp olive oil
3 tsp ground cumin
2 tbsp curry powder, or to taste, depending on strength
3 cloves garlic, peeled and crushed
1 onion, finely chopped
2 tbsp freshly grated root ginger
Salt and freshly ground black pepper
675g minced beef or lamb
Ketchup, to serve

1. Heat 5 tablespoons of the olive oil and fry the spices together with the garlic, onion, ginger and seasoning for about 2–3 minutes.
2. Place the meat in a bowl and add the fried spices and vegetables. Mix together well, then shape and press into 50 small balls.
3. Fry the balls in the remaining oil for about 7 minutes in batches of 15–20, moving them continually while frying to prevent sticking.
4. When they are well browned and cooked thoroughly, keep warm and serve together with the ketchup.

## SPICY DIPS

Cocktail koftas, sausages and chicken nuggets all taste better if they are served with a good spicy sauce.

For a quick way of making these, use mayonnaise, quark, or low-fat soft cheese or Greek yoghurt as the base. Simply add a little tomato ketchup and chilli powder; mango chutney and curry powder; Worcestershire sauce and your favourite relish; or a mixture of ground cumin and freshly chopped coriander.

**TIP**

Cocktail food should not really be very messy, but some items can be a little greasy, so have plenty of small paper napkins to hand.

# MIXED MINI BURGERS

Keep these mini burgers really small for a canapé buffet or make slightly larger ones to serve in small sesame buns at a finger buffet. Secure the latter with a cocktail stick.

**Makes 30**

**To serve**
60 small rounds (4cm diameter) fried bread (any)
American cucumber relish

## BEEF BURGERS

**450g minced beef**
**2 tbsp very finely chopped onions**
**1 clove garlic, peeled and crushed**
**1 tbsp tomato ketchup**
**1 tsp Worcestershire sauce**
**1 teaspoon mixed dried herbs**
**Salt and freshly ground black pepper**
**1 tbsp olive oil**

1. Place all the ingredients, except the olive oil, in a bowl and mix together well with a fork. Shape into small balls with a teaspoon.
2. Heat the olive oil in a large frying pan and place half the beef balls in the pan. Press down each one with a fork to make into a mini hamburger. Fry on each side for about 2–3 minutes until cooked through.
3. Drain on kitchen paper and repeat the process with the second batch of beef balls.

# LAMB BURGERS

**450g minced lamb**
**2 tbsp very finely chopped celery**
**1 tbsp freshly chopped parsley**
**6 dried apricots, very finely chopped**
**Salt and freshly ground black pepper**
**1 tbsp olive oil**

1. Place all the ingredients, except the olive oil, in a bowl and mix together well with a fork. Shape into small balls with a teaspoon.
2. Heat the olive oil in a large frying pan and place half the lamb balls in the pan. Press down each one with a fork to form a mini hamburger. Fry on each side for about 2–3 minutes until cooked through.
3. Drain on kitchen paper and repeat the process with the second batch of lamb balls.

**To serve**
Place one mini burger on each round of fried bread and top with a little dollop of American cucumber relish.

# CHILLI CON CARNE SPOONS WITH GUACAMOLE

Larger quantities of this recipe can also be used to make chilli con carne for a fork buffet. It is up to you how much chilli you use but not everyone is keen on very hot food, so keep the quantity down for a canapé buffet and perhaps increase the amount for a buffet menu where there is a choice of another dish.

**Serves 45–50 in spoons**

**1 tbsp olive oil**
**150g finely chopped onions (approx. 2 large onions)**
**1 cloves garlic, peeled and finely chopped**
**1–1½ tbsp dried chilli powder to taste**
**300g minced beef**
**1 x 400g tin tomatoes**
**100ml beef stock**
**1 tsp dried oregano**
**½ level tsp ground cumin**
**Salt and freshly ground black pepper**
**1 x 200g tin red kidney beans, drained**
**150g guacamole**

**1.** Heat the oil in a large pan, add the onions and garlic and fry for 2–3 minutes. Add the chilli powder and continue cooking for a further minute or two. Add the minced beef, making sure that any clusters of meat are broken up. Cook over a medium heat, stirring from time to time, for about 5–6 minutes.

2. Add the contents of the can of tomatoes, stock, oregano, cumin and seasoning. Return to the boil. Turn down the heat and simmer for about an hour; the mixture should be bubbling gently all the time.

3. Add the drained beans and check the levels of chilli and seasoning, adding more if necessary. Return to the boil and simmer for a further 15–20 minutes. The mixture should be quite thick. If it is too runny, turn up the heat for a short while to boil off the excess liquid.

4. Leave to stand for at least an hour before reheating and serving.

5. To serve, place small spoonfuls in Chinese porcelain soup spoons and top with a small dollop of guacamole.

# DEEP-FRIED SMOKED TROUT BALLS

Use this simple base to make various kinds of fish balls with cooked white fish or chopped prawns in place of smoked trout.

**Makes 50**

500g smoked trout, mashed
2 large floury potatoes, peeled, cooked and mashed
2 egg yolks
1 clove garlic, peeled and crushed
2 tbsp freshly chopped parsley or dill
Salt and freshly ground black pepper
Plain flour
Cooking oil, for deep-frying

1. Remove any bones from the fish and process in a blender with the potatoes, egg yolks, garlic and herbs. Season to taste. Take care not to over-process or the mixture will go sticky.
2. Shape into 50 small balls. Roll in plain flour and deep-fry in hot oil for 4–5 minutes until brown and crispy. Drain on kitchen paper and serve at once with tartare sauce on the side.

# TAPENADE CATHERINE WHEELS

This is another versatile recipe, which can be used to make larger wheels for finger food or smaller wheels for canapé menus.

**Makes 40-50**

**2 x 400g shortcrust pastry**
**Plain flour, for rolling out**
**300g tapenade, black or green olive paste**

1.  Preheat the oven to 190°C/375°F/Gas 5.
2.  Roll out half the pastry on a floured surface/board to make a rectangle about 26 x 18cm.
3.  Spread with half the tapenade or olive paste and roll up along the long side into a Swiss roll. Transfer to a tray and chill in the fridge for an hour or store in the freezer.
4.  Cut the roll into 20–25 slices and arrange on a baking tray. Bake for about 5–10 minutes until lightly browned. Serve at once or cool on a wire rack to keep on one side and reheat later in the day. Repeat with the remaining pastry and olive paste.

# SAVOURY CHEESE TRUFFLES

Surprise your guests by covering both savoury mixtures with all the coatings.

**Makes 50**

350g full-fat soft cheese
225g Edam cheese, grated
225g water biscuits, finely crushed
175g Danish blue cheese
50g walnuts, chopped
100g dates, chopped
Grated rind of 2 oranges
4 tbsp tomato relish
Mayonnaise (optional)

*Coatings*
Toasted sesame seeds
Poppy seeds
Finely chopped parsley or basil

*Decoration*
8 sprigs fresh basil

1. Mix the soft cheese, Edam and water biscuits together in a bowl. Divide the mixture in half: mix one half with the blue cheese and walnuts and the other half with the remaining ingredients. Add a touch of mayonnaise to either mixture if it shows signs of being crumbly.
2. Take teaspoonfuls of both mixtures and shape into small balls with your hands. Coat well in one of the coatings and spear with cocktail sticks. Garnish with sprigs of fresh basil.

# FINGER BUFFETS

Finger food is designed to be more substantial than canapés. It offers a way of giving quite a large number of people a good meal in a confined space. It is not meant to be a cop-out for people who cannot afford to put on a proper spread! A finger buffet is a very useful style of catering if you only have a small house or flat and do not want to hire an outside venue. The food can be laid out on quite a small table or it can be handed round by friends or waitresses and so avoid completely the need for large buffet tables.

A finger buffet is also practical because the food is not as fiddly and time-consuming to make as canapés. The items will be more substantial and will not need individual garnishes; with finger food it is the tray or platter that needs the garnish. On top of this, fewer helpers will be needed to assist with the preparation and in handing the food round, and there will be less laying out, clearing away and washing-up.

## THE PLAN

Start by looking at the catering master checklist on (pages 5–6) and work through it, adding the relevant sections to your own checklist.

Here are some extra points to consider as you go along.

# THE VENUE

Much the same considerations will apply to a finger buffet as to a canapés and drinks reception (see page 31). Your own home will probably hold quite a large number of standing guests or you could hire a local hall or club.

Calculate the standing space in your venue on the basis of about 1 square metre per person, making allowances for buffet and drinks tables. Remember that elderly people do not like to stand for too long, so set aside a room or an area with chairs for older members of the family.

# THE FOOD

The food must be easy to eat with the fingers and this means that there will probably be quite a few bread- and pastry-based items. These can be backed up with small pieces of meat such as chicken wings and small lamb cutlets, sausages, satay and stuffed eggs and vegetables.

A mixture of hot and cold items is always attractive. It also means that the cold items can be prepared well in advance and stored under cling film in a cool place. Hot items can be prepared in advance and reheated or prepared and cooked on the spot.

Quite a lot of items can be bought-in ready-made from the chilled or frozen food cabinets and, although they cost a little more than home-made items, they can help to ease the workload. Other interesting items can be bought from take-away restaurants or delicatessens.

The best way to plan quantities is to take a dinner plate and imagine how many items of finger food would fill it. The answer will probably be about eight or nine. You might allow two rather than one per person of very small items such as breaded scampi or cocktail sausages.

## IDEAS FOR READY-MADE FOOD TO BUY IN

BASICS:
- Sausages and small sausage rolls
- Vol-au-vent cases
- Barbecued and hot & spicy chicken wings
- Breaded scampi
- Mini buffet pork pies
- Pizzas cut into pizza fingers
- Ready-made quiches cut into squares
- Baby lamb cutlets

MORE FUN ARE:
- Satay sticks
- Indian samosas and pakora
- Chinese spring rolls
- Greek filo pastry parcels
- Falafel
- Crispy duck parcels
- Mini croissants to stuff

You may also want to introduce some sweet items to a finger buffet menu.

IDEAS INCLUDE:
- Mini-cupcakes
- Individual profiteroles
- Mini-meringues

- Chocolate truffle cups
- Small tartlets

The choice of menu will dictate how much work there will be to do on the day. A lot of food can be made in advance. Sandwiches with drier fillings can be made the day before and stored in the fridge overnight, well sealed in cling film. Pastries with moist fillings will have to be left to the last minute, but the pastry and the filling can both be made in advance and stored separately.

### SAUSAGES

Hot or cold sausages are probably the most popular buffet food after smoked salmon. You simply cannot go wrong with them. Choose small cocktail sausages and serve whole or buy large ones and cut in half or into lengths.

There are all kinds of sausages to choose from. Try a mixture of pork, beef and Cumberland or look out for some of the more interesting flavoured herb and garlic sausages. Spicy Merguez and Vienna sausages are another possibility.

Serve the sausages with mustard or a spicy sauce or split lengthways and top with grated cheese and chutney, corn or tomato relish, or Worcestershire sauce and chopped tomatoes. Pop under the grill for a few minutes just before serving.

# FINGER BUFFET MENU 1

This is a simple menu that includes quite a large proportion of ready-made items.

## MENU

COLD

Green Goddess Dip (pages 110–11) and Camembert and
  Caraway Dip (page 111) with crudités and nachos
Asparagus Rolls (page 118)
Black and White Double-deckers (pages 116–17)
Smoked Chicken, Avocado and Cranberry Open Sandwiches
  (page 115)
Marinated Lamb Cutlets with Spicy Sauce (pages 143–44)

HOT

Mini samosas
Sausage rolls
Barbecue chicken wings
Scampi with garlic dip

BUY IN READY-MADE

Smoked chicken
Mini samosas
Sausage rolls
Barbecue chicken wings
Scampi
Garlic dip

## PLAN

PREPARATION EARLIER IN THE DAY AND COVER IN CLING FILM

- Make the black and white double-deckers; store in a cool place
- Make the green goddess dip and Camembert and caraway dip, and prepare the crudités; store in the fridge
- Make the asparagus rolls, pack into plastic boxes and store in the fridge
- Cook the lamb cutlets and leave to cool; store in the fridge
- Make the spicy sauce for the lamb cutlets and store in a cool place
- Make the open sandwiches and store in a cool place

AT THE LAST MINUTE

- Heat the sausage rolls and samosas in the oven
- Heat the barbecue chicken wings
- Cook the scampi

# FINGER BUFFET MENU 2

This is a more elaborate buffet that involves more preparation, so make sure you have enough help in the kitchen. You may need two ovens if you have a large number of guests.

## MENU

COLD
Quick Tomato and Tuna Dip (page 110) with crudités
Lebanese Cheese Dip (page 112) with Baked Pitta Bread
  Dippers (page 113)
Smoked salmon on black bread
Ham and Tongue Rolls (page 120)
Stuffed Vegetable Platter (page 126)

HOT
Satay Sticks with Peanut Sauce (page 140)
Sausages with tomato relish
Squares of Smoked Salmon and Courgette Dill Quiche (page 134)
Spiced Chicken Wings and Drumsticks (page 142)
Scampi with tartare sauce

SWEET
Chocolate Truffle Cups (page 148)

## PLAN

BUY IN READY-MADE
• Sausages
• Tomato relish

- Scampi
- Tartare sauce

## PREPARE IN ADVANCE
- Prepare the tomato and tuna dip; store in the fridge
- Make home-made chicken liver pâté for stuffed vegetables and store in the fridge
- Prepare two other fillings for stuffed vegetables and store in the fridge
- Make the chocolate truffle cups and store in a cool place

## PREPARE EARLIER IN THE DAY AND COVER IN CLING FILM
- Make Lebanese cheese dip and store in the fridge
- Prepare stuffed vegetable platter and store in a cool place
- Prepare ham and tongue rolls; store in the fridge
- Prepare smoked salmon on black bread and store in the fridge
- Put satay to marinate and make peanut sauce; store in a cool place
- Prepare quiche base and filling; store in a cool place
- Marinate the chicken wings and store in a cool place

## AT THE LAST MINUTE
- Cook spiced chicken wings and drumsticks and sausages
- Arrange dips and crudités on platters
- Grill satay sticks and heat up the peanut sauce
- Finish off and cook the quiche
- Bake the pitta bread
- Deep-fry the scampi
- Arrange truffle cups on platters

# FINGER BUFFET MENU 3

This is a vegetarian menu that is quite heavy on preparation.

## MENU

COLD
Stuffed Eggs Oriental (page 130)
Chicory Spears with Orange-spiced Tabbouleh (page 128)
Choux Puffs (pages 136–7) filled with Guacamole (page 59)
Stuffed Vegetable Platter (page 126)
Asparagus Rolls (page 118)

HOT
Cheese Dreams (page 139)
Baby vegetable samosas
Domino Tortilla Squares (page 138)
Falafel with tahini dip
Squares of Wild Mushroom Quiche (pages 132–3)

SWEET
Mini-meringues (page 149)

## PLAN

BUY IN READY-MADE
• Baby vegetable samosas
• Falafel and tahini paste
• Guacamole (optional)

PREPARE IN ADVANCE
- Make and bake the choux puffs and store in an airtight tin
- Make and bake the mini-meringues and store in an airtight tin
- Make the wild mushroom quiche base and store in a cool place
- Make the guacamole, if not using ready-made, and store in the fridge

PREPARE EARLIER IN THE DAY AND COVER IN CLING FILM
- Make the chicory spears with tabbouleh and store in a cool place
- Hard-boil the eggs, cool and stuff; store in a cool place
- Make the stuffed vegetable platter and store in a cool place
- Prepare and cook the tortilla and store in the fridge
- Make the asparagus rolls; pack in a box and store in a cool place
- Prepare the cheese dreams and store in the fridge

AT THE LAST MINUTE
- Finish off and bake the quiche
- Fill the choux puffs with the guacamole
- Put the meringues together
- Reheat the tortilla, heat the falafel and baby samosas
- Mix tahini paste with water to make a dip
- Cook the cheese dreams

# FINGER BUFFET MENU 4

This is a summer barbecue buffet. The preparation is relatively simple but, depending on the number of guests, you will probably need extra help cooking the food on the barbecue.

## MENU

TO EAT WHILE THE BARBECUE IS GETTING GOING
Mixed crostini: Porcini Crostini (page 73), Chopped Liver Crostini (page 129) and Italian Bruschetta with Herbs (page 63)

COOKED ON THE BARBECUE
Lamb Cutlets with various marinades (pages 143–4)
Skewered Potatoes with Spinach Dip (page 114)
Sausages with grainy mustard
Oriental-style Chicken Drumsticks (page 145)
Grilled sweetcorn

TO ACCOMPANY THE GRILLED FOOD
Salad Kebabs (page 127)

## PLAN

BUY IN READY-MADE ITEMS
• Grainy mustard
• Sausages
• Sweetcorn

## THE DAY BEFORE

- Prepare the marinades for the lamb cutlets
- Place the lamb cutlets in the marinades and store in the fridge
- Prepare the porcini and chopped liver crostini toppings; store in the fridge
- Prepare and pre-cook the chicken drumsticks; store in the fridge

## PREPARE EARLIER IN THE DAY AND COVER IN CLING FILM

- Make the spinach dip and store in the fridge
- Cook the potatoes and keep on one side
- Pre-cook the sausages to finish off on the grill
- Prepare the Italian tomato crostini topping
- Cut the heads of sweetcorn into four chunks and pre-cook
- Prepare the salad kebabs and store in the fridge

## AT THE LAST MINUTE

- Slice the ciabatta loaves and toast on the barbecue; serve with the three toppings while the rest of the meal is cooking
- Cook the lamb cutlets, sausages and chicken drumsticks on the barbecue
- Finish the potatoes and sweetcorn on the barbecue

# FINGER BUFFET MENU 5

This is an afternoon teatime buffet. You may not need so much help for this type of buffet as most of the sweet items can be made in advance, leaving the savoury items to prepare on the day.

## MENU

SAVOURY
Seafood Open-Sandwich Selection (pages 121–2)
Double-decker Sandwiches on Skewers (pages 123–5)
Asparagus Rolls (page 118)

SWEET
Scones with clotted cream and jam
Coffee Éclairs (page 151)
Chocolate-iced Cupcakes (page 153)
Malakoff Cake (page 152)

## PLAN

BUY IN READY-MADE
• Prawn cocktail
• Scones
• Clotted cream
• Jam

THE DAY BEFORE
• Bake the éclair choux puffs and prepare the filling and store separately

- Prepare and bake the cupcakes (without icing) and store in an airtight tin

## PREPARE EARLIER IN THE DAY AND COVER IN CLING FILM
- Prepare the toppings for the seafood open sandwiches and store in the fridge.
- Make the Malakoff cake and store in the fridge
- Ice the cupcakes
- Make the asparagus rolls and keep cool and moist
- Make the double-decker sandwiches and keep cool and moist

## AT THE LAST MINUTE
- Make up the seafood open sandwiches
- Split the scones and top with clotted cream and a little jam
- Fill the éclairs
- Cut the Malakoff cake

## THE DRINKS

Champagne or sparkling wine throughout is the easiest, though perhaps not the cheapest, option for a finger buffet event. However, a choice of red and white wine will be quite acceptable. If you are planning a wedding reception during the day, chose lighter wines – your guests will not thank you for a thick head on the way home (see page 18 for drinks suggestions).

## THE EQUIPMENT

You should not need too much in the way of special equipment for a finger buffet. See page 29 for a checklist for the Finger Buffet Menu given on page 97. However, if you are planning a barbecue buffet you will certainly need to borrow or hire another one or two barbecues to add to your own if the numbers are more than 8–10.

Remember that you will also need corkscrews, paper napkins, a knife for the cake, if there is one, and ashtrays. An afternoon tea buffet may also necessitate special equipment such as cake stands, cake forks and teacups and saucers.

## STAFF AND HELPERS

Both the hot and the cold food can be left on a buffet table, but if you do have enough helpers it is probably better to hand the food around. This helps to ensure everyone gets a fair share. Otherwise, those nearest the buffet table do rather well while those by the door or on the other side of the room may miss out.

You will need at least one helper to serve food to 20 people and the drinks need to be served as well. So allow two helpers to

30–35 guests. Remember, you may also need some help in the kitchen to replenish the serving platters and to heat or cook the hot food. At a barbecue buffet helpers will be needed in order to keep the food coming and avoid long delays between each batch.

# THE RECIPES

## DIPS WITH CRUDITÉS

Colourful dips with fresh crudités are a real eye-catcher on any buffet. Choose two or three contrasting dips and offer to guests to keep hunger at bay as the party warms up.

**Serves 24-30**

### CRUDITÉS

Choose three or four vegetables from the list below. Think about the combination of colours on the serving platter and the different textures to offer a really interesting mix.

**2 each red, green and yellow peppers, seeded and cut into strips**
**1 cucumber, cut into sticks**
**4 large carrots, cut into sticks**
**24 long radishes**
**1 head cauliflower, broken into florets**
**3 heads chicory, separated into spears**
**450g raw mangetout, sliced once lengthways**

**1.** Arrange on a large plate and serve with the dips.

> **TIP**
> If you want to make the crudités in advance, toss the carrots in lemon juice and cover the whole plate with cling film and store in a cool place.

## QUICK TOMATO AND TUNA DIP

This is a very quick dip to make and it goes particularly well with celery, cucumber and chicory dippers. Use the drained tomato juice in spicy sauces.

**Serves 15-20**

2 x 200g tins tuna, drained
600g tined tomatoes, very well drained
350g low-fat soft cheese or quark
1 bunch spring onions, finely chopped
2 small green chillies, seeded and finely chopped
½ x 2.5ml pack dried mixed herbs

*Decoration*
Paprika
2 spring onions, sliced

1. Mix all the ingredients together in a bowl.
2. Garnish with paprika and spring onion.

## GREEN GODDESS DIP

This is a very English version of the American dip. It goes well with mixed pepper sticks and celery. You could also add some grissini or breadsticks to the choice of dippers.

**Serves 15-20**

3 bunches watercress, very finely chopped
1 clove garlic, peeled and crushed
6 tbsp freshly chopped mint

**1kg Greek yoghurt**
**Salt and freshly ground black pepper**
**Paprika and sprigs of mint, for decoration**

1. Place all the ingredients in a food processor and blend well together, or mash with a fork and mix well.
2. Decorate with paprika and springs of mint.

## CAMEMBERT AND CARAWAY DIP

For a really colourful effect, serve this dip with cauliflower florets, strips of red and green peppers and mangetout.

**Serves 20**

**2 x 350g wheels Camembert cheese**
**225g low-fat soft cheese or quark**
**6 tbsp dry white wine**
**2 tsp caraway seeds**
**Salt and freshly ground black pepper**

1. Cut the thick rind off the corners of the cheese. Slice the remaining cheese into pieces and place in a blender or food processor.
2. Add the soft cheese, wine, caraway seeds and seasoning and blend until smooth.

## LEBANESE CHEESE DIP

Serve with baked Pitta Bread Dippers (see opposite).

**Serves 10**

**225g feta cheese**
**1 tbsp water**
**Juice of 1 lemon**
**2 tbsp olive oil**
**1 red Italian or mild onion, finely chopped**
**½ large cucumber, peeled and diced**

*Decoration*
**Sprigs of continental parsley**
**Black olives**

1. Mash the cheese in the water with a fork.
2. Add the lemon juice and then the oil, still mixing with a fork. Finally, stir in the onion and cucumber.
3. Garnish with parsley and olives.

---

**TIP**

If you do not want to go to the trouble of making your own dips the supermarkets offer a wide range ready-made. Houmous, guacamole, Greek tzatziki and taramasalata quickly spring to mind but there are many other more adventurous dips from which to choose.

# BAKED PITTA BREAD DIPPERS

If you have a large number of guests, make all three variations and present on a board.

**Makes about 30**

**1 bag of 5 or 6 pitta breads**
**3–4 tbsp olive oil**
**5 tbsp sesame seeds**

1. Preheat the oven to 200°C/400°F/Gas 6.
2. Brush the pitta bread all over with olive oil. Place on a baking tray and sprinkle liberally with sesame seeds. Cut each pitta bread into five or six long thin sticks.
3. Bake for 5–6 minutes until crisp and golden. Serve at once.

## VARIATIONS

- Use a mixture of 3–4 tablespoons corn or sunflower oil and a few drops of Chinese roasted sesame oil
- Use half and half corn or sunflower oil and walnut oil, and sprinkle with black poppy seeds.

# SKEWERED POTATOES WITH SPINACH DIP

If you have the time and the workforce, make up more elaborate vegetable kebabs by adding small pieces of cooked red pepper and cocktail onions to the cocktail sticks before adding the cooked potatoes.

**Makes 50**

**25 small to medium size new potatoes**

*Spinach dip*
**500g frozen chopped spinach**
**6 tbsp freshly chopped parsley**
**250ml mayonnaise**
**Salt and freshly ground black pepper**

1. Cook the new potatoes in boiling water until tender. Drain and leave to cool.
2. Cut in half and skewer each half with a cocktail stick. Cook on the barbecue, cut side down. Allow the cut surface to sear slightly with parallel grill marks.
3. To make the spinach dip, thaw the spinach and drain very well, pressing against the sides of a sieve. Turn into a basin and mix in all of the remaining ingredients, seasoning to taste. Add a little more mayonnaise if the mixture is too thick.
4. Serve the barbecued potatoes with the dip.

# SMOKED CHICKEN, AVOCADO AND CRANBERRY OPEN SANDWICHES

The secret with open sandwiches is to give some height to the topping. Do not just lay pieces of chicken and avocado flat on the butter. Raise them up with a piece of lettuce and arrange one just a little differently. Avoid the temptation to add too many garnishes.

**Makes 45**

**45 x 6cm square pieces of firm wholemeal or rye bread**
**150g butter, softened**
**45 small pieces of lettuce**
**600g (4 breasts) smoked chicken fillets, cut into small slices**
**3 large ripe avocados, cut into small slices**

*Garnish*
**Cranberry sauce**
**Sprigs of fresh parsley and chervil**
**Freshly ground black pepper**

1. Spread butter on each of the bread squares.
2. Place a small piece of lettuce on each one. Arrange a slice of smoked chicken and one of avocado on top of the lettuce. Garnish with a small teaspoonful of cranberry sauce and a tiny sprig of parsley or chervil.
3. Sprinkle with freshly ground black pepper.

# BLACK AND WHITE DOUBLE-DECKERS

These multi-coloured double-decker sandwiches look most attractive on a white plate. Garnish with a scattering of capers or pomegranate seeds.

**Makes 48**

24 slices small white sliced loaf, crusts removed
12 slices German pumpernickel black bread
450g liver sausage or homemade Chicken Liver Pâté (page 49)
2 tbsp dried sage
Salt and freshly ground black pepper
350g cooked beetroot, grated
175g dill cucumber, finely diced
2 tbsp mayonnaise
Capers or pomegranate seeds, for decoration

1. Cut the white bread to the same size as the black bread.
2. Mix the liver sausage or pâté with the sage, salt and pepper.
3. Blend the remaining ingredients with a little salt and pepper in another basin.
4. Place a slice of white bread on a board and spread with the liver sausage or pâté mixture.
5. Spread a slice of pumpernickel with the beetroot mixture and place on top of the liver sausage or pâté mixture. Top with another slice of white bread. Cut into 4 small sandwiches.
6. Continue filling the remaining slices of bread in the same way and then pack into a rigid polythene container or wrap in foil. Store in the fridge until required.

## ALTERNATIVE FILLING

**8 eggs, beaten**
**25g butter**
**6 tbsp milk**
**Salt and freshly ground black pepper**
**100g smoked salmon, chopped**
**225g lettuce leaves, shredded**
**2 tbsp mayonnaise**

1. Scramble the eggs with the butter and milk. Season to taste and leave to cool. Mix in the smoked salmon.
2. Mix the lettuce and mayonnaise together, and season. Proceed as above.

---

**TIP**

People do like to know what they are eating and it is not always easy to tell what is in a sandwich by looking at it. So it's a good idea to prepare labels. Stick them to cocktail sticks and skewer into the mound of sandwiches. You could do the same for quiche and pizza squares.

# ASPARAGUS ROLLS

These little rolls are quick and easy to make and extremely popular, so consider making double quantities.

**Makes 36**

**2 small brown loaves**
**100g butter, softened**
**36 asparagus spears, drained canned, or fresh or frozen, cooked**

1.  Slice the loaf as thinly as possible, buttering as you go. Cut off the crusts.
2.  Place an asparagus spear on the buttered side of each piece of bread and roll up. Place in a polythene box and cover with the end crusts of the loaf to keep the rolls from drying out.
3.  Cover and store in the fridge or freezer until required.

## ALTERNATIVE FILLINGS

**50 slices cold roast beef**

1. Cut the meat into six pieces and roll up each piece fairly tightly. Cut each roll in half.
2. Proceed as page 118.


**225g Cheddar cheese, grated**
**225g carrots, grated**
**1 tbsp mayonnaise**
**Salt and freshly ground black pepper**

1. Mix all the ingredients together in a basin.
2. Make a mound of the mixture along one edge of the piece of bread and roll up. Repeat until all of the filling has been used.


**TIP**

To cut fresh bread really thinly, dip the bread knife into a jug of boiling water between cutting each slice.

# HAM AND TONGUE ROLLS

This is really a similar idea to the Asparagus Rolls but sliced meat is used instead of the thinly sliced brown bread.

**Makes 50**

**13 square slices ham, trimmed of all fat**
**12 slices tongue**

*Fillings*
**675 g low-fat soft cheese**
**3 sweet/sour pickled cucumbers, very finely chopped**
**1 tbsp mild mustard**
**3 tbsp mango or other chutney**
**Salt and freshly ground black pepper**

*Decoration*
**Cherry tomato halves**
**Continental or English parsley**

1. Start by making the two fillings: beat the soft cheese with the cucumber and divide into two portions. Mix the mustard into one half and the chutney into the other. Mix each filling thoroughly and season to taste.
2. Spread the mustard-flavoured mixture over the slices of ham. Roll up and cut each roll in two.
3. Trim the slices of tongue into square and rectangular shapes. Chop the trimmings and add to the chutney-flavoured filling. Spread this filling over each slice of tongue and roll up. Cut each roll in two.
4. Place both ham and tongue rolls on a serving plate and garnish with cherry tomato halves and parsley.

# SEAFOOD OPEN SANDWICHES

A selection of these sandwiches arranged together on a board looks very attractive. The original Danish open sandwich uses rye bread and this gives a good firm base to the sandwich, but you can use any kind of bread to hand. Keep the sandwich bases small for afternoon tea, around 5cm square.

**Makes 30 (each recipe)**

## SMOKED SALMON ON CAPER CHEESE

150g thick-cut smoked salmon, cut into strips about 8 x 3cm
150g cream cheese
2 tbsp capers, finely chopped
1 tbsp finely chopped spring onion
Salt and freshly ground black pepper
30 x 5cm square pieces of rye bread
100g butter, softened
5 hard-boiled eggs, sliced
Capers or caper berries, for garnish

1. Prepare the salmon strips and roll up into small rolls.
2. Mix the cream cheese with the capers and spring onion and season to taste. Spread each square of bread with butter and then with the caper cheese.
3. Arrange a slice of hard-boiled egg and a salmon roll on top of the cheese and garnish with a few whole capers or one caper berry.

## PRAWN COCKTAIL WITH ASPARAGUS

30 x 5cm square pieces rye bread
100g butter, softened
30 small, centre leaves from 4–5 gem lettuces
300g prawn cocktail
30 spears asparagus, canned or cooked

1. Spread each square of bread with butter and press a small lettuce leaf or half a leaf into the butter to secure it in place.
2. Top with small spoonfuls of the prawn cocktail mix. Arrange an asparagus tip on top of the prawns.

## GRAVADLAX WITH MUSTARD CHEESE

150g cream cheese
2 tbsp grainy mustard
Freshly ground black pepper
30 x 5cm square pieces rye bread
100g butter, softened
2 pickled cucumbers, sliced very finely
150g gravadlax, cut into small pieces
Small sprigs of dill, for garnish

1. Mix the cream cheese with the mustard and black pepper.
2. Spread each square of bread with butter and then with the mustard cheese. Arrange a slice of cucumber, slightly folded to give height to the sandwich, on top of the cheese, and then add a piece of gravadlax, also folded slightly.
3. Garnish with tiny sprigs of dill.

# DOUBLE-DECKER SANDWICHES

Use small cocktail sticks to hold these double-decker sandwiches together. Choose two or three different fillings to make a mixture of sandwiches.

**Makes 32 (each recipe)**

## EGG AND CHICKEN WITH TARRAGON FILLING

**8 eggs, beaten**
**50g butter, softened**
**40ml water**
**40ml milk**
**3 tsp dried tarragon**
**Salt and freshly ground black pepper**
**4 cooked chicken breast fillets**
**16 slices white bread, crusts removed**
**8 slices brown bread, crusts removed**
**2 tbsp mayonnaise**

1. Start by scrambling the eggs with 50g of the butter, the water, milk and tarragon, taking care to keep the eggs soft. Season to taste and leave to cool.
2. Slice the chicken breasts.
3. Butter half the slices of white bread and all the brown bread on one side. Lay out the buttered slices of white bread and spread with the tarragon egg mixture. Top with the slices of brown bread and arrange the sliced chicken on this layer.
4. Spread the remaining white bread with the mayonnaise and lay mayonnaise-side down on the chicken.
5. Cut each double-decker sandwich into four smaller sandwiches and secure with a cocktail stick.

## HAM AND PICKLE FILLING

**200g mayonnaise**
**100g gherkins, very finely chopped**
**8 caper berries, very finely chopped**
**2–3 spring onions, trimmed and very finely chopped**
**150g butter, softened**
**16 slices white bread, crusts removed**
**Salt and freshly ground black pepper**
**400g ham, sliced**
**8 slices brown bread, crusts removed**

1. Mix the mayonnaise with the gherkins, caper berries and spring onions and season to taste.
2. Butter half the slices of white bread and lay out on a board. Top with the sliced ham.
3. Butter the brown bread and place, buttered side down on the ham. Spread the mayonnaise pickle on the brown bread and top with the remaining slices of white bread.
4. Cut each double-decker into four small sandwiches and secure with cocktail sticks.

## TUNA, CHEESE AND CRESS FILLING

3 x 114g tin tuna, drained and mashed
35g walnuts, finely chopped
¼ small onion, finely chopped
Salt and freshly ground black pepper
3 tbsp mayonnaise
1 box cress
200g soft cheese, such as Philadelphia
150g butter, softened
16 slices white bread, crusts removed
8 slices brown bread, crusts removed

1. Mix the tuna with the walnuts, onion, seasoning and mayonnaise.
2. Mix the cress with the soft cheese.
3. Generously butter all the slices of bread on one side. Lay half the slices of white bread butter-side up on a board. Spread with the tuna mixture. Top with the brown bread, butter-side down.
4. Spread on the cheese and cress mixture and top with the remaining white bread, butter side down.
5. Cut each double-decker into four smaller sandwiches and secure with cocktail sticks.

# STUFFED VEGETABLE PLATTER

Raw vegetables stuffed with a variety of fillings make very colourful platters for a finger buffet.

## VEGETABLES

**Red, green and yellow peppers:** Remove the stalks and seeds from the peppers and cut into quite large squares.

**Small open-cup mushrooms:** Remove the stalks to the level of the tip of the mushroom; if you remove the stalk completely you may find that water will stay in the base after they are rinsed.

**Celery:** Wash the stalks and cut into 5–7cm lengths.

**Tomatoes:** Cut in half around the centre, or cut with a zigzag pattern to give a floral effect. Spoon out the seeds using a teaspoon.

**Cucumber:** Cut in half lengthways and then cut into 3cm lengths. Scoop out the seeds with a teaspoon.

## FILLINGS

Cream cheese flavoured with freshly chopped herbs, watercress or cress

Home-made Chicken Liver Pâté (page 49)

Liver sausage on its own or flavoured with freshly chopped sage or thyme

Scrambled eggs flavoured with freshly chopped tarragon

Mashed sardines in tomato sauce

Smoked cod's roe mixed with cream cheese

Canned tuna mixed with very finely chopped celery and walnuts and a little mayonnaise

# SALAD KEBABS

These crunchy cold kebabs make a refreshing accompaniment to a barbecue buffet but they can also be served as part of other finger buffets. Make up two or three combinations and mix these on the serving platters.

Cherry tomatoes
Basil leaves
Small celery sticks

Squares of green peppers
Apricot quarters
Pieces of chicory spears

Cubes of cucumber
Cocktail onions
Squares of red peppers

Cubes of carrot
Sprigs of curly parsley
Radishes

Apple wedges
Mint leaves
Squares of yellow peppers

**1.** Make up cocktail sticks with two of each item on each stick.

# CHICORY SPEARS WITH ORANGE-SPICED TABBOULEH

Try to buy small heads of chicory as the outer leaves can be very big.

**Makes 50**

6–7 heads chicory, leaves separated
175g bulgur wheat
1 x 225g tin mandarin orange segments
8 tbsp freshly chopped parsley
Grated rind of 2 oranges
½ small red pepper, seeded and finely chopped
5 tbsp extra virgin olive oil
4 tbsp lemon juice
½ tsp cinnamon
½ tsp ground coriander
Salt and freshly ground black pepper

1. Arrange the chicory leaves on a large serving plate.
2. Place the bulgur wheat in a bowl and cover with plenty of boiling water. Leave to stand for 30 minutes. Drain very well, squeezing out all the water with your fingers.
3. Drain the mandarin orange segments very well on kitchen paper. Chop and mix with the bulgur and all the remaining ingredients. Place a spoonful of this mixture onto each spear of chicory.

# CHOPPED LIVER CROSTINI TOPPING

Freshly toasted ciabatta slices make a great base for do-it-yourself crostini. As soon as the barbecue is ready to use, grill a batch of slices and offer them round for guests to spread with their own choice of topping from bowls on the buffet table. Grill more batches of bread as the event proceeds.

**Makes sufficient to top around 30 slices**

**3 onion, sliced**
**500g lamb's liver, in one piece**
**3 tbsp water**
**3 hard-boiled eggs**
**Salt and freshly ground black pepper**

1. Preheat the oven to 180°C/350°F/Gas 4.
2. Place half the sliced onion in the base of a small ovenproof dish. Add the lamb's liver and water and then the remaining onion. Cover and bake for 45 minutes.
3. Cut the liver into pieces and mince or process in a food processor with the onions and 1 tablespoon of the cooking liquor.
4. Rub the eggs through a sieve, add to the mixture and season to taste. Leave to cool and then chill in the fridge before serving in a bowl.

# STUFFED EGGS ORIENTAL

This traditional party standby takes on a new look when you employ some Eastern flavours.

**Makes 48**

**24 hard-boiled eggs or 50 quail's eggs, shelled**
**150ml mayonnaise**
**Salt and freshly ground black pepper**
**2 tbsp mango chutney**
**2 tsp mild curry powder**
**2 tbsp freshly chopped coriander**
**Small bunch spring onions, chopped**
**Sprigs of fresh coriander, for decoration**

1. Cut the eggs in half lengthways, carefully remove the yolks and place in a basin. Mash with a fork and add the mayonnaise and seasoning, mixing well.
2. Divide the mixture in two and mix one half with the mango chutney and curry powder and the other half with the chopped coriander and spring onions.
3. Pile the fillings back into the empty egg whites. Place on a large plate and garnish with sprigs of fresh coriander.

## VARIATIONS

Instead of mango chutney, curry powder and coriander, try 6–8 tablespoons freshly chopped parsley or 1 box cress and 1 teaspoon paprika.

**TIP**

For a canapé buffet use quail's eggs in place of hen's eggs. Quail's eggs can be difficult to peel. Use eggs which are a week old. Roll the eggs on the worksurface to crack the shells all over, then peel under running water. You can, of course, solve the whole problem by buying jars of ready-cooked and peeled quail's eggs.

# AS-YOU-LIKE-IT QUICHE

People never seem to tire of quiche, and you can certainly ring the changes by adding different flavouring ingredients to the basic eggs, cheese, milk and cream. Quiches are useful both as finger food and on a cold buffet.

Here are two large quiches to try, with variations.

## WILD MUSHROOM QUICHE

Use dried wild mushrooms or Italian porcini to give a really strong flavour to this quiche. Soak them in boiling water for about half an hour before using and keep the soaking liquid to flavour other dishes.

**Serves 12**

225g shortcrust pastry
Plain flour, for rolling out
25 dried wild mushrooms
225g flat mushrooms, wiped and sliced
50g chopped walnuts
100g Cheddar cheese, grated
3 eggs
150ml single cream
75ml milk
Salt and freshly ground black pepper

1. Preheat the oven to 190°C/375°F/Gas 5.
2. Roll out the pastry on a floured surface/board and use to line a 27–28cm flan dish. Line with foil and fill with dried beans or lentils and bake for 10 minutes. Remove the foil and beans and then bake for a further 5 minutes.
3. Sprinkle mushrooms and walnuts evenly over the base of the flan and add the cheese.
4. Beat the eggs, cream and milk together with the seasoning and pour over the top. Return to the oven and bake for 45–50 minutes until golden on top and set in the centre. Serve hot or cold, cut into triangular slices.

## VARIATIONS

In place of the mushrooms and walnuts try one of the following:

- 450g frozen leaf spinach, thawed, drained and mixed with butter and nutmeg
- 2 x 225g tins asparagus tips, well drained
- 175g sweetcorn kernels and ½ large red pepper, seeded and diced
- 350g grated carrot, softened in butter

## SMOKED SALMON AND COURGETTE DILL QUICHE

**Serves 16-18**

This was a favourite when I was running my catering company in London. Try to buy offcuts of smoked salmon rather than the full pieces. You will be cutting up the smoked salmon and it works out much cheaper this way.

**225g shortcrust pastry**
**Plain flour, for rolling out**
**225g smoked salmon pieces, roughly chopped**
**4 medium-sized courgettes, thinly sliced**
**150g Cheddar cheese, grated**
**4 eggs, beaten**
**150ml single cream**
**150ml milk**
**Salt and freshly ground black pepper**
**2 tbsp freshly chopped dill**

1. Preheat the oven to 190°C/375°F/Gas 5.
2. Roll out the pastry on a floured board/surface and use to line a 31 x 23cm Swiss roll tin. Line with foil and fill with dried beans or lentils and bake for 10 minutes. Remove the foil and beans and then bake for a further 5 minutes.
3. Sprinkle the chopped smoked salmon over the base of the flan and add the courgette slices and cheese. Mix the eggs, cream and milk with the seasoning and pour over the top. Sprinkle the chopped dill over the top.
4. Return to the oven and bake for 50–55 minutes until golden on top and set in the centre. Serve hot or cold, cut into small squares.

## VARIATIONS

In place of the smoked salmon and courgettes use one of the following:

- 225g cooked and flaked smoked haddock and sliced tomatoes
- 225g diced cooked ham or bacon with 100g cooked peas
- 75g blue cheese, such as Stilton or Roquefort, mixed with 1 large sliced onion, softened in butter
- 225g cooked chicken mixed with 100g sweetcorn kernels

# CHOUX PUFFS

Choux puffs are really very easy to make and they are also very versatile as you can fill them with savoury or sweet fillings. Use this mixture, too, to make a choux ring by piping onto a circle drawn on baking paper.

**Makes 50**

300ml water
100g butter, chopped, plus extra for greasing
150g plain flour
Pinch of salt
4 eggs

1. Preheat the oven to 200°C/400°F/Gas 6 and meanwhile grease a baking tray.
2. Heat the water in a saucepan with the butter until the butter melts and the water comes to the boil. Quickly stir in all the flour and the salt and beat vigorously until the mixture is smooth and leaves the sides of the pan.
3. Remove from the heat and beat in the eggs, one at a time, beating well after each addition. The final paste should be thick and shiny.
4. Place 50 small spoonfuls onto baking trays and bake for 20 minutes. Reduce the heat to 190°C/375°F/Gas 5 and bake for a further 10–15 minutes until well-cooked. Lift out onto a wire rack and split open with a sharp knife to allow the steam to escape. Leave to cool.
5. These puffs, or profiteroles, may be served cold or they can be reheated in the oven and filled with a hot filling. They freeze well or can be stored in an airtight tin for a short time.

## SUGGESTED FILLINGS

- Salmon or seafood mousse
- Cream cheese flavoured with herbs or mixed with chopped smoked salmon, smoked mackerel or trout, or with chopped ham, tongue or prawns
- Whipped cream; plain or flavoured with chocolate, coffee or a liqueur
- Ice-cream

# SPANISH TORTILLA SQUARES

A tortilla is a thick Spanish omelette, which in Spain is usually served cold, cut into chunky squares. It makes a filling and tasty finger food.

**Makes 48**

1 onion, sliced
2 tbsp olive oil
450g potatoes, peeled and grated
2 large eggs, beaten
Salt and freshly ground black pepper
½ tsp turmeric

1. Fry the onion in 1 tablespoon olive oil until lightly browned. Mix with the grated potato, eggs, seasoning and turmeric.
2. Heat the remaining olive oil in a 20cm non-stick frying pan. Pour in the potato mixture; it should be about 2cm thick. Cook over a medium to low heat for 10–15 minutes until the top is almost set and then finish off under the grill.
3. Loosen the sides and leave to cool in the pan. Cut into squares and serve.

## VARIATIONS

### DOMINO TORTILLA

Add small squares of fried red, green and yellow peppers to the potato mixture.

### MEATY TORTILLA

Add diced chorizo sausages to the potato mixture.

# CHEESE DREAMS

This is another very simple idea, which simply walks off the plates!

**Makes about 24 squares**

**24 thin slices white bread, crusts removed**
**22g butter, softened**
**450g Cheddar cheese, grated**
**6 tbsp sweet pickle or chutney**
**2–3 tsp olive oil**

1. Thinly butter the slices of bread, setting aside the remaining butter.
2. Mix the cheese with pickle or chutney and spread the mixture over 12 of the bread slices. Top with the remaining slices to make 12 sandwiches.
3. Cut each sandwich diagonally to make four small triangular sandwiches.
4. Heat the remaining butter and the oil in a frying pan until fairly hot. Fry the triangles in the mixture for 2–3 minutes on each side, turning over as they crisp up and the cheese begins to foam. Quickly brown on the second side and serve piping hot.

# SATAY STICKS WITH PEANUT SAUCE

Any kind of meat can be used for these satay sticks, though pork and chicken are traditional.

**Makes 50**

1kg lean pork, cut into 1cm cubes
300ml plain yoghurt
Juice and grated rind of 2 lemons
2 cloves garlic, peeled and crushed
8 chicken breast fillets or 12 boned chicken thighs, cut into 1cm cubes
50 thin wooden skewers, soaked in water

*Peanut sauce*
1 x 350g jar, crunchy or smooth peanut butter
175ml milk, plus extra if needed
2 tbsp soy sauce
100g creamed coconut, chopped

1. Place the prepared pork in a bowl. Mix together the yoghurt, lemon juice and rind, and crushed garlic and pour half over the pork. Stir and leave to stand in the fridge for at least an hour.

2. Use the remaining yoghurt mix to marinate the chicken in the fridge.

3. Thread the meats onto the wooden skewers, retaining the marinade. Cook the satay in batches under a moderate grill for about 6–8 minutes, turning from time to time.

4.  To make the sauce, beat the remains of the marinade into the peanut butter. Pour the milk into a small pan and add the soy sauce and creamed coconut, then stir over a low heat until all the coconut has dissolved.

5.  Add the peanut butter mixture to the pan and beat until well mixed. Add more milk if necessary, to keep the mixture smooth and creamy. Bring to the boil, turn down the heat and cook for 5 minutes, continuing to add milk if the sauce thickens too much.

# SPICED CHICKEN WINGS
# AND DRUMSTICKS

Drumsticks can be treated in much the same way to make more
substantial finger food – use 25–30 in place of the wings.

**Makes 100**

**50 chicken wings, cut in half**
**450ml plain yoghurt**
**2 tbsp freshly grated root ginger**
**4 cloves garlic, peeled and crushed**
**1 tbsp turmeric**
**1 tsp ground cumin**

1. Preheat the oven to 190°C/375°F/Gas 5.
2. Skin the chicken wings as much as possible.
3. Mix all the remaining ingredients together and pour over the
   chicken. Leave to marinate in a shallow dish or bowl for at
   least an hour.
4. Arrange on baking trays and bake for 30 minutes.

---

**TIP**

A very quick way of preparing both wings and drumsticks is to
sprinkle them with a liberal seasoning of mixed herbs, freshly
ground black pepper, grated lemon rind and salt. Bake in a high
oven with the skin still in place. Drain off any fat halfway through
the cooking time.

# MARINATED LAMB CUTLETS FOR THE BARBECUE

The marinades give really different flavours to the lamb, so if you choose to offer two different flavours, make sure that the serving platters are labelled accordingly. French-cut racks of lamb are the best choice for the barbecue as there is very little fat on them to flare up the flames. Of course, in the winter the cutlets could be cooked under the grill in the kitchen. The cutlets will take about 3–4 minutes to cook on each side.

**Makes about 48**

**6 French-cut racks of lamb, cut into about 48 cutlets**

Choose one of the following marinades:

## ORANGE AND TARRAGON MARINADE

**4 tbsp orange marmalade**
**Juice and grated zest of 1 orange**
**Juice of 1 lemon**
**100ml white wine**
**50ml olive oil**
**Freshly ground black pepper**

1. Mix all the ingredients well together in a saucepan and place over a low heat to dissolve the marmalade.
2. Allow to cool, then pour over the cutlets.
3. Leave to stand in a cool place until required for the barbecue.

## RED WINE AND GARLIC MARINADE

100ml red wine
100ml extra virgin olive oil
½ small onion, finely chopped
4 cloves garlic, peeled and crushed
1 bay leaf
Freshly ground black pepper

1. Mix all the ingredients well together and pour over the cutlets.
2. Leave to stand in a cool place until required for the barbecue.

## INDIAN MARINADE

3 tbsp olive oil
1 onion, finely chopped
1 clove garlic, peeled and crushed
4 tbsp medium curry powder
1 heaped tsp ground cumin
1 heaped tsp ground coriander
1 level tsp ground cardamom
2 tbsp concentrated tomato purée
300ml water

1. Heat the oil in a pan and gently fry the onion and garlic for a minute or so.
2. Stir in the curry powder and spices. Add the tomato purée and then the water. Bring to the boil, stirring all the time. Reduce the heat and leave to simmer gently for 15 minutes.
3. Allow to cool, then pour over the cutlets.
4. Leave to stand in a cool place until required for the barbecue.

# ORIENTAL-STYLE CHICKEN DRUMSTICKS

These drumsticks can be prepared well in advance and stored in the freezer until required. Thaw overnight in the fridge.

**Makes 50**

**50 small drumsticks**
**Juice and zest of 5 large oranges**
**300ml strong soy sauce**
**3 level tsp five-spice powder**
**Plenty of black pepper**

1. Cook the drumsticks in batches: Arrange 10–12 drumsticks in a large shallow frying pan with a lid.
2. Mix all the remaining ingredients and pour over the chicken. Cover with the lid and bring to the boil. Reduce the heat and simmer the chicken in the sauce, turning from time to time. Depending on their size, the drumsticks will take about 20-30 minutes to cook through.
3. Leave to cool and then pack in plastic boxes with the cooking juices and freeze.
4. To cook on the barbecue, thaw in the fridge overnight. Place on the barbecue and grill until the skins are crispy; this does not take very long.

# MINTED LAMB TARTLETS

These delicious little meat pies are well worth the effort it takes to make them. Your guests will be impressed.

**Makes 28**

**3 tbsp olive oil**
**1 large onion, finely chopped**
**1kg minced lean lamb**
**115ml lamb or chicken stock**
**1 small bunch mint, freshly chopped**
**4 tbsp redcurrant jelly**
**Salt and freshly ground black pepper**
**1kg shortcrust pastry**
**Plain flour, for rolling out**
**1 egg, beaten**

1. Preheat the oven to 220°C/425°F/Gas 7.
2. Heat the oil and cook the onion until soft. Add the lamb and brown.
3. Stir in the stock and simmer for 20 minutes. Add the mint, redcurrant jelly and salt and pepper and leave to cool.
4. Roll out the pastry on a floured surface to line 28 x 7.25cm bun tins and cut out 28 lids. Fill with the lamb mixture and cover with the pastry lids. Glaze with beaten egg and bake for 15 minutes. Serve hot or cold.

# PINEAPPLE AND COCONUT CHEESECAKE

Cheesecakes are easy to make and can be cut into squares to serve at a finger buffet or into triangles to serve at a fork buffet or sit-down meal. You can use any kind of biscuits in this versatile flan base. Just add a little more sugar if using unsweetened biscuits.

**Serves 12**

25g cornflakes, crushed
50g biscuits, crushed
25g desiccated coconut
75g granulated sugar
100g butter, melted

*Filling*
300ml pineapple juice
150g creamed coconut, chopped
1 x 12g sachet powdered gelatine
350g cottage cheese
4 tbsp desiccated coconut, toasted under the grill

1. Mix together the crushed cornflakes, biscuits, coconut, sugar and melted butter. Press into the base of a 25cm loose-based flan tin and place in the fridge.
2. Heat 3–4 tablespoons pineapple juice in a pan and stir in the creamed coconut. When the coconut has melted, keep over a low heat and sprinkle on the gelatine. Stir until dissolved; do not allow the mixture to boil. When the gelatine has dissolved, remove from the heat and stir in the rest of the pineapple juice.
3. Pour into a blender or food processor and blend with the cottage cheese. Pour the mixture into the prepared base. Leave to cool then return to the fridge to set. Sprinkle the top with toasted coconut just before serving.

# CHOCOLATE TRUFFLE CUPS

These chocolate cups also make very good petits fours for a sit-down menu.

**Makes 36**

**225g plain chocolate**
**36 paper sweet cases**

*Filling*
**175g plain chocolate, chopped**
**50g butter**
**1 egg yolk**
**Grated rind of 2 oranges**
**2 tbsp orange liqueur**
**100g crushed sweet biscuits**
**50g walnuts, chopped**
**8 glacé cherries, finely chopped**
**Walnut halves, for decoration**

1. To make the chocolate cases, melt the chocolate in a bowl set over barely simmering water in a pan, stirring occasionally. Place a teaspoon of chocolate in a paper case and, using a pastry brush, spread all over the sides of the case. Repeat with the remaining cases, then chill until set.

2. To make the filling, melt the chocolate in a bowl as above. Add the butter and egg yolk and then beat in the remaining ingredients. Leave to cool a little, then pile into the set chocolate cases.

3. Decorate the tops with walnut halves and chill until required. To serve, remove from the paper cases.

# MINI-MERINGUES

These tiny cocktail meringues make a deliciously sweet mouthful to finish off the feast. Use up the egg yolks to glaze vol-au-vents or to make mayonnaise. Of course, this recipe can also be used to make regular-size meringues.

**Makes 24**

6 egg whites
250g caster sugar
50g soft brown sugar
6 tbsp lemon curd
300ml double cream, whisked to soft peaks
50g icing sugar
2 tsp crème de menthe

1. Preheat the oven to 120°C/250°F/Gas ½. Cover two baking trays with baking parchment.
2. Whisk the egg whites until stiff. Gradually add 200g of the caster sugar and continue to whisk until very stiff. Divide the mixture in two. Add the remaining caster sugar to one batch and fold in. Fold the brown sugar into the other batch.
3. Pipe tiny whirls of each type of meringue onto the prepared trays and place in the oven to dry out. This will take about 1–1½ hours.
4. Mix the lemon curd with half the cream and use to sandwich half the meringues together.
5. Mix the remaining cream with crème de menthe and icing sugar and use to fill the rest of the meringues.

# ITALIAN BAKED CHEESECAKE

This cheesecake cuts easily into quite thin wedges, which can be served at a finger buffet, or it may be cut into small squares to add a sweeter item to a canapé buffet.

**Makes 16-20 small slices**

**200g ricotta cheese**
**175g cream cheese**
**2 tbsp pine nuts, toasted**
**1 tbsp raisins**
**1 tbsp flour**
**3 eggs, beaten**
**Juice of ½ lemon**
**1 tsp vanilla essence**
**50g sugar**

*Base*
**150g biscuit crumbs**
**75g butter, softened**

1. Preheat the oven to 190°C/375°F/Gas 5 and lightly grease a 20cm diameter, loose-based, sponge cake tin.
2. To make the base, mix together the biscuit crumbs and butter and press into the bottom of the prepared cake tin.
3. Mix the two cheeses with the pine nuts, raisins and flour in a large bowl. Beat the eggs with the lemon juice, vanilla essence and sugar in a separate basin. Gradually add to the cheese mixture and combine in three or four batches. Mix well together and pour into the prepared cake tin.
4. Bake for 40 minutes until cooked through; a knife should come out clean when cut into the centre.
5. Ease round the sides of the cheesecake with a palette knife to release any sticking to the tin. Leave to cool for 5 minutes before removing from the tin. Leave to fully cool on the tin base before cutting.

# COFFEE ÉCLAIRS

These traditional teatime treats are very popular, but are quite quick and easy to make.

**Makes 35**

**Choux Puffs (see page 136–7)**

*Coffee filling*
**6 eggs**
**75g cornflour**
**1.25 litres milk**
**300g caster sugar**
**6 tbsp instant coffee**
**1 tsp vanilla essence**

*Icing*
**6 tbsp espresso coffee or a mixture of instant coffee and sherry**
**300g icing sugar**

1. Start by making the éclairs using the choux puff recipe on pages 136–7 and piping 35 long éclairs (rather than 50 round puffs).
2. To make the filling, beat one egg with the cornflour to make a paste and gradually add the remaining eggs.
3. Heat the milk and stir in the sugar, coffee and vanilla essence. Just before the mixture boils, remove from the heat and stir 100ml into the egg mixture. Transfer back to the pan containing the remaining liquid and stir over a low heat until you have a thick custard. Leave to cool.
4. Pipe a little of the coffee filling into the centre of each éclair.
5. To make the icing, carefully add the coffee and sherry, if using, to the icing sugar. Quickly spread a little along the centre of the top of each éclair.

# MALAKOFF CAKE

This is an easy cake to make as it requires no baking, but it looks very impressive nonetheless. Make the day before you plan to serve it, as it needs to be chilled for at least 6 hours. You could use up the egg whites by making Mini-Meringues (see page 149).

**Serves 8**

125g unsalted butter
125g caster sugar
3 egg yolks
125g ground almonds
600ml double cream, whipped
35–40 boudoir biscuits
2 tbsp brandy
3 tbsp toasted flaked almonds

1. Beat the butter until soft and then beat in the sugar. Beat in the egg yolks, one at a time. Finally stir in the almonds and a quarter of the cream.
2. Place a layer of boudoir biscuits on the base of an 18cm loose-based cake tin and sprinkle with 1 tablespoon brandy. Spread a layer of almond cream over the top and cover with whipped cream. Add another layer of boudoir biscuits and the rest of the brandy. Continue with almond cream and whipped cream and biscuits until used up, ending with a layer of cream.
3. Decorate with the toasted almonds.

# CHOCOLATE-ICED CUPCAKES

You can use this recipe for all kinds of cupcakes – just substitute another flavouring for the chocolate and add 50g ground almonds.

**Makes 24**

**4 eggs**
**225g butter**
**225g caster sugar**
**275g plain flour**
**100g cocoa powder**
**2 tsp baking powder**
**50–60ml milk**

*Chocolate butter icing*
**225g butter, softened**
**400g icing sugar**
**100g cocoa powder**
**Milk**

*Decoration*
**Chocolate vermicelli**

1. Preheat the oven to 180°C/350°F/Gas 4 and arrange 24 non-stick cupcake cases on a baking tray or grease 2 x 12-bun trays.
2. To make the cake mixture, place all the ingredients, except the milk, in a food processor and process quickly together. Add sufficient milk to make a smooth dropping consistency.
3. Fill the cupcake cases or bun trays with the mixture and bake for 15–20 minutes. Leave to cool
4. To make the butter icing, beat all the ingredients together, adding sufficient milk to give a spreading consistency. Spread over the top of the buns.
5. Decorate with chocolate vermicelli.

# FORK BUFFETS

A fork buffet can mean anything from a simple quiche and salad to a table of traditional cold cuts, an array of vegetarian foods or a selection of the finest haute cuisine dishes. The choice is yours.

This type of buffet is less formal than a full-scale sit-down meal, but you still have the choice of either providing seating for your guests or leaving them standing and so packing in a larger number.

The cost and workload of a fork buffet are decided very much by your choice of menu. You could, if money is no object, decide to go for a shellfish buffet with lobster and crab. Alternatively, you might offer an attractive but economical spread based on a selection of quiches and flans, and there are any number of choices in between. The menus in this section don't include ready-made dishes – there are not many that you can buy in sufficient quantities for this type of buffet, and what is available is anyway not as good as home-made.

## THE PLAN

Start by looking at the event master checklist on pages 5–6. Work through it, adding the relevant sections to your own checklist.

Here are some extra points to consider as you go along.

## THE VENUE

Most of the venues you might choose for a canapés and drinks reception or for a finger buffet can usually also be used for a fork buffet, but you will need to allow a little more space. You will need a good-sized buffet table and room for everyone to get to it. The individual space allowance per person will also need to be larger as it takes more elbow room to juggle with a plate and fork as well as a glass.

Elderly people prefer to sit down to eat and this is even more important for them at a fork buffet than it is at a finger buffet. You may, of course, decide that everyone should be able to sit down. If so, you will need to calculate the space needed for people seated at tables or for chairs placed around the room for your guests to eat off their laps, in addition to the buffet table.

## THE FOOD

Almost anything goes on a good buffet table, but texture and colour do become very important. Try to visualise all the dishes you are planning on the table together. How do they look? Does the spread need any more colour? Are there too many rather similar dishes and is there a contrast of crunchy and creamy dishes?

Unless you are providing seating for everyone, the golden rule is to avoid serving food which needs to be cut up. This means that chicken on the bone, steaks, chops and the like are out at a stand-up buffet. Salmon is manageable as it flakes easily with a fork. Cold cuts such as turkey, ham and tongue can be served if they are very tender and sliced into pieces that do not need to be cut more than once or twice with a fork.

Other factors that will affect the choice of food are the number of guests and the likely temperature of the room. If the numbers are large, go for dishes which are quick to serve rather than those that are fiddly to dish up or take time to carve. There is nothing more irritating to guests than having to queue up for ages waiting to be served.

The room temperature could affect aspic coatings or render salad garnishes limp, and it would certainly not be a good idea to serve salmon mousse or ice-cream gateaux if there are no fridges on site in which to store them until they are served.

## QUANTITIES

Most people like to try everything that is on a buffet so allow a small portion for each guest. Do make sure that dishes such as pies and terrines are already cut into portions or detail a waitress or helper to serve small portions. You do not want anything to run out before all the guests have arrived at the table.

Two or three main dishes will usually be sufficient if they are backed up with a filler such as potatoes or rice, either hot or in salad form, and a couple of vegetables or green salads. It is probably worth remembering that if people are serving themselves they will probably only take one spoonful of these items.

A fork buffet can be made up of two, three or even four courses. Usually the main course is supplemented by an interesting choice of desserts and, however much people say they are slimming or on a diet, the desserts still seem to disappear. A starter or appetiser can also be served, but unless you go for a chilled soup or a fruit or prawn cocktail, I think it is better incorporated into the general spread. For example, if a guest prefers to keep shellfish and meat separate, then they can come to the buffet table a second time.

## ACCESS TO THE BUFFET

Make sure that it is easy for people to get to and from the buffet. If there are a large number of guests you may want to repeat all the dishes to form two complete sections on the buffet. You can set it up to offer access along both sides of the table or with two starting points at either end of one side.

# FORK BUFFET MENU 1

This is a traditional summer fork buffet, which is probably more suitable for sitting than for standing. However, if you decide on a standing buffet serve the vichyssoise in small teacups. The cost of this buffet is relatively modest and the preparation fairly easy.

## MENU

Vichyssoise (page 175)
Dressed Salmon (pages 170–2) with Coriander and Chervil
  Potatoes (page 199)
Grape and Paprika Chicken (page 185)
Spring Vegetable Salad (page 202)
Russian Salad (page 198)
Strawberry Feather Cake (pages 218–9)
Summer Fruit Platter (page 212)

## PLAN

PREPARE IN ADVANCE
- Cook the sponge cakes for the strawberry feather cake. Store in a tin
- Prepare the vichyssoise and store in the freezer

PREPARE EARLIER IN THE DAY AND COVER IN CLING FILM
- Cook the salmon, cool and dress; store in the fridge
- Make the grape and paprika chicken; store in a cool place
- Prepare and cook the coriander and chervil potatoes; store in a cool place
- Prepare the spring vegetable salad and store in a cool place

- Prepare the Russian salad and store in the fridge
- Thaw the vichyssoise and store in the fridge

AT THE LAST MINUTE
- Arrange the salmon, grape and paprika chicken on large serving platters
- Arrange salads on large serving platters
- Prepare the summer fruit platter
- Put the strawberry feather cake together

# FORK BUFFET MENU 2

This hot buffet menu is suitable for standing or sitting. The preparation is fairly straightforward but time-consuming.

## MENU

Crab and Egg Cocktails (page 177)
Creamy Fish Pie with Scalloped Potatoes (pages 188–9)
Beef in Red Wine (pages 250–1) and rice
Mixed vegetable selection
Tipsy Trifle (pages 214–5)
Normandy Apple Tart (page 213)

## PLAN

### PREPARE IN ADVANCE

- Prepare and cook beef in red wine and store in the freezer

### PREPARE EARLIER IN THE DAY AND COVER IN CLING FILM

- Thaw the beef in red wine and store in the fridge
- Prepare creamy fish pie and scalloped potatoes; store in the fridge
- Prepare vegetables and store in a cool place
- Bake the Normandy apple tart
- Prepare the tipsy trifle and store in the fridge
- Prepare the ingredients for crab and egg cocktails; store in the fridge

## AT THE LAST MINUTE

- Finish off the crab and egg cocktails
- Cook the creamy fish pie with scalloped potatoes
- Reheat beef in red wine
- Cook the rice and vegetables

# FORK BUFFET MENU 3

This is a hot pasta-based fork buffet suitable for standing or sitting. There is quite a lot of last-minute preparation and you may need help in the kitchen for the meal itself. Remember when assessing quantities that people often like to try smaller portions of each of the pasta dishes rather than take a full portion of just one.

## MENU

Moulded Cucumber Salads with Horseradish Cream (page 176)
Fusilli with Prawn and Herb Sauce (page 203)
Spinach, Ricotta and Feta Lasagne (pages 206–7)
Buttons and Bows Pasta (page 204)
Mixed leaf salad with vinaigrette dressing
Raspberry Shortcakes (page 222)
Pineapple and Orange Stars (page 210)

## PLAN

PREPARE IN ADVANCE
- Make the moulded cucumber salads and horseradish cream the day before; store in the fridge
- Cook the shortcakes and store in a tin

PREPARE EARLIER IN THE DAY AND COVER IN CLING FILM
- Prepare the lasagne to just before baking
- Prepare the ingredients for the buttons and bows pasta
- Prepare the salad and vinaigrette and store in the fridge
- Prepare the pineapple and orange stars and store in a cool place

AT THE LAST MINUTE
- Bake the lasagne in the oven
- Cook the farfalle pasta and finish with the sauce and meatballs
- Cook the fusilli and prepare the prawn and herb sauce; toss together
- Toss the salad with the vinaigrette dressing
- Finish off the raspberry shortcakes
- Unmould the cucumber salads onto small individual plates; pipe on the horseradish cream

# FORK BUFFET MENU 4

This is a cold vegetarian menu suitable for standing or sitting. Most of the preparation can be carried out in advance on the day rather than just before the meal.

## MENU
Gazpacho (page 174)
Sun-dried Tomato and Goats' Cheese Tart (pages 182–3)
Old-fashioned Egg Flan (page 187)
Cheese Log (page 186)
Rainbow Pasta Salad (page 205)
Mushroom and Sweetcorn Salad (page 201)
Banana and Orange Charlotte (page 217)
Fruit salad with mangoes and kiwifruit

## PLAN

PREPARE IN ADVANCE
• Make the gazpacho and store in the freezer
• Prepare the tart and flan bases; store in the freezer

PREPARE EARLIER IN THE DAY AND COVER IN CLING FILM
• Prepare and chill cheese log; store in the fridge
• Cook pasta and make the rainbow pasta salad; store in a cool place
• Make the banana and orange charlotte; store in a cool place
• Thaw pastry bases
• Prepare and bake sun-dried tomato and goats' cheese tart
• Scramble the eggs for the old-fashioned egg flan

- Make mushroom and sweetcorn salad; store in a cool place
- Thaw gazpacho (and prepare accompaniments); store in the fridge
- Prepare the fruit salad and store in the fridge

AT THE LAST MINUTE
- Prepare gazpacho garnishes
- Put the scrambled egg flan together
- Arrange cheese log
- Fill and decorate egg flan

# FORK BUFFET MENU 5

This elaborate cold buffet is suitable for a standing or a sit-down meal. A good deal of the preparation for this menu can be done in advance.

## MENU

Seafood Mousse (pages 178–9)
Pork and Herb Terrine (pages 180–1)
Roast Gammon with Redcurrant Glaze and Cloves (page 194)
Decorative Charcuterie Platter (page 192)
Fruity Rice Salad (page 209)
Waldorf Salad (page 197)
Mediterranean Roasted Vegetable Salad (page 200)
Orange Cassata Bombe (pages 220–1)
Yorkshire Curd Tarts (page 216)

## PLAN

PREPARE IN ADVANCE
- Roast the vegetables for the Mediterranean salad
- Prepare and cook Pork and Herb Terrine; store in the freezer
- Roast the gammon and store in the freezer
- Bake the Yorkshire curd tarts and store in the freezer
- Make the orange cassata bombe and store in the freezer

PREPARE EARLIER IN THE DAY AND COVER IN CLING FILM
- Prepare and cook the seafood mousse; store in the fridge
- Thaw any frozen items
- Slice the terrine and decorate; store in the fridge

- Carve and decorate the gammon; store in a cool place
- Arrange the charcuterie platter and store in a cool place
- Cook rice and prepare fruity rice salad; store in the fridge
- Make the Mediterranean vegetable salad and store in a cool place

AT THE LAST MINUTE
- Turn out seafood mousse and decorate
- Finish off the Mediterranean roasted vegetable salad
- Prepare Waldorf Salad

## THE DRINKS

Choose the wines to go with a fork buffet in just the same way as you would if it was a sit-down meal (see page 18), but avoid wines that are very heavy if the reception is at midday.

## THE EQUIPMENT

Both trestle tables for the buffet and round tables at which the guests can sit may be hired from catering equipment hire companies, as can chairs, tablecloths and the like. You will probably also need to hire crockery, cutlery and glasses. It is possible to manage with a single plate, fork and glass per person, but this really is very minimal and only suitable for the simplest buffet. For anything more sophisticated, see the checklist under Hiring Equipment on pages 28–9.

Standing up and juggling a plate, fork and glass at the same time can be difficult. But help is at hand in the form of glass holders, which can be clipped to the side of your plate, thus freeing one hand to hold the plate and the other to wield the fork. And your guests won't keep losing their glasses this way.

If you are planning to have hot food, you can also hire bain-marie units or burner warmers, which will keep the food hot while it is being served and save you having to bring it out in batches.

## STAFF AND HELPERS

The number of kitchen helpers you need will depend very much on the number of guests you have invited and upon the ease or difficulty of your chosen menu. For waiting staff, allow one waitress or helper to twelve or fourteen guests.

# THE RECIPES

## SALMON

This is one of the most popular buffet dishes of all time, especially during the summer months when wild salmon was available. Today salmon is farmed and so is on sale all year round, but it has not lost its appeal.

Order fresh salmon in advance from your local fishmonger or from the wet-fish counter in the supermarket. When you collect the fish, check that it is resilient and firm to the touch. The skin should have a natural sparkle and the eyes should be full and bright.

Salmon is quite a filling food and 75g of cooked salmon will make a very good portion. After allowing for the head and the bones, this means that an uncooked 3kg salmon will serve 15 people.

### POACHED SALMON

This is really the best way to cook salmon. If you follow these instructions to the letter, you can be sure of never overcooking the fish. If you do not have a fish kettle you may be able to borrow one from a friend or hire one from a catering-equipment hire company.

Place the cleaned fish in a fish kettle and cover with water. Add one sliced onion and one sliced carrot, together with 2 tablespoons each of olive oil and white wine or lemon juice, a bay leaf, a sprig of parsley and a dozen black peppercorns.

Cover with a lid and bring to the boil over a medium heat. Stand over the fish and when the liquid starts to boil properly, time the fish to boil for *one minute* only. Turn off the heat. Leave to cool for 25 minutes if serving hot or to cool completely in the cooking liquor.

This method and timing works with any size of fish because the larger the fish, the longer the water will take to come to the boil and to cool afterwards.

## BAKED SALMON

If you do not have a fish kettle you may be able to get a whole salmon in your oven. Take care, though, because it is easy to overcook the fish with this method.

Clean and season the fish, and wrap loosely in very well-oiled foil. Place on a tray and bake in a preheated oven at 180°C/350°F/Gas 4. Allow 13–15 minutes per 450g.

## MICROWAVED SALMON

This can be useful for smaller fish. Prepare as for baking and wrap well-oiled in cling film. Allow 2–3 minutes per 450g on full power; check with your microwave handbook before cooking as power levels vary.

## PRESENTING THE SALMON

To serve the fish, lift it out of the liquid and place on a serving dish. Ease the skin off one side and flip over using two fish slices. Remove the skin on the second side. Mop up any liquid round the fish with kitchen paper.

You may leave the head and tail in place or remove them, depending on how you feel. If you leave the head in place cover the eye with some of the garnish. Simple decorations include overlapped slices of cucumber or piped rosettes of mayonnaise. Both these methods can be used to disguise the fact that you have had to cut the salmon in half to get it into your oven or microwave.

Cucumber tends to dry up quite quickly, so brush with oil or, if you have time, cover with a thin layer of aspic. For a wedding, cover the fish with a muslin cloth while you are at the church or registry office and remove when you get home. Add some lettuce leaves or sprigs of watercress or parsley if you think the fish looks a little bare on its own.

Flavoured butter goes well with hot salmon, and flavoured mayonnaise with cold salmon. Try mixing freshly chopped dill, parsley or tarragon into the butter or mayonnaise.

# RICE, PASTA AND POTATOES

Most people cook far too much of these accompaniments to the main course. Here's a general guide to follow. You may need to add a little more per person for sit-down meals. Somehow people seem to take less when they are standing up.

Rice: Allow 40g per person, uncooked rice
Pasta: Allow 30–40g per person, uncooked pasta
New potatoes: Allow 100g per person, unpeeled raw potatoes
Mashed potato: Allow 100–150g per person, peeled raw
  potatoes

## COOKING RICE

A surprising number of people say they cannot cook rice. In fact, it is quite easy if you follow the rules carefully.

### TO COOK 1 KG LONG-GRAIN RICE

1. Place the rice in a large pan or Dutch oven. Boil 2 litres water and pour over the rice. Place on a high heat and return to the boil. Stir once and cover with a lid, reduce the heat and simmer for 15–20 minutes.
2. Leave to stand for 5 minutes. Remove the lid and check the rice at the base of the pan. If it is a little sticky, cook for a further 3–5 minutes on a low heat and stand for another 3 minutes.
3. Fluff up with a fork and serve or use cold in salads.

Alternatively, bake the rice with boiling water in a casserole with a lid at 190°C/375°F/Gas 5 for 45–50 minutes until all the liquid has been absorbed and the rice is cooked through.

# GAZPACHO

This popular dish originated in Andalucia, Spain, where the tomatoes are so ripe they don't need the added tomato purée.

**Serves 30**

**2kg very ripe tomatoes, skinned, seeded and chopped**
**3 red peppers, seeded and chopped**
**1 large cucumber, chopped**
**3 tbsp finely chopped onion**
**1 tbsp finely chopped garlic**
**200ml wine vinegar**
**90ml tomato purée**
**900ml water**
**150ml extra virgin olive oil**

*Garnishes*
**6 slices thick-cut white bread, crusts removed, diced and**
  **fried in olive oil**
**1 medium red pepper, skinned, seeded and diced**
**1 cucumber, diced**
**Ice cubes**

1. To make the soup, purée all the vegetable ingredients in a food processor or blender with the vinegar. Mix the tomato purée with the water and stir into the soup with the oil; chill for at least two hours.
2. Prepare the garnishes and store under cling film until required. Serve with ice cubes floating in the soup and the garnishes in separate bowls.

# VICHYSSOISE

This is a classic summer favourite, served with dill croutons, which is easy to make for large numbers and economical too. Use a really good chicken stock for the best flavour, adding a little more at the end if the soup is too thick. Double up the quantities for a large party.

**Serves 30**

**1.5kg trimmed and finely chopped leeks**
**750g floury potatoes, peeled and cubed**
**1.5 litres good chicken stock**
**500ml milk**
**Salt and freshly ground black pepper**
**100ml double cream**

*Garnish*
**8 slices white bread, crusts removed**
**75g butter**
**1 tbsp olive oil**
**Small bunch fresh dill, coarsely chopped**

1. Place the chopped leeks in a large saucepan with the potatoes, chicken stock, milk and seasoning. Bring to the boil, then reduce the heat and simmer for 30 minutes. Leave to cool and store in the fridge or freezer.

2. To make the dill croutons, fry the slices of white bread in batches in the butter and olive oil until they are golden in colour; take care not to brown the butter. Leave the bread to cool and cut into tiny cubes.

3. Just before serving, stir the cream into the vichyssoise and top each bowl with the fried bread croutons and a pinch of chopped dill.

# MOULDED CUCUMBER SALADS
# WITH HORSERADISH CREAM

These little light salads can be made the day before and stored in the fridge. Serve on small individual plates.

**Makes 20**

3 x 25g packets aspic jelly
1 tbsp gelatine powder
Juice of 6 lemons
1.2 litres boiling water
1.2 litres white wine
4 cucumbers, grated
1 large onion, grated
3 tbsp capers, chopped
Black pepper

*Horseradish cream*
125ml double cream
1 tbsp grated horseradish
Salt and freshly ground black pepper

1.  Mix the aspic and gelatine with the lemon juice and pour over the boiling water. Stir until the aspic and gelatine are dissolved. Add the white wine and leave to cool.
2.  Mix all the remaining ingredients together and pour onto the aspic mixture. Spoon into 24 individual moulds – small pudding moulds or ramekin dishes are suitable – and place in the fridge to set.
3.  To make the horseradish cream, whip the cream into stiff peaks and stir in the grated horseradish and seasoning. Place in a piping bag.
4.  Just before serving, turn the cucumber salads out onto small plates and pipe a rosette of horseradish cream on the side.

# CRAB AND EGG COCKTAILS

To achieve the best results for this dish, it is important to pick over the crab meat really carefully to remove any bits of bone or cartilage.

**Serves 24**

12 hard-boiled eggs, chopped
1kg white crab meat, carefully picked over
500ml mayonnaise
2 tbsp lemon juice
3 tbsp tomato ketchup
1 tbsp Worcestershire sauce
Salt and freshly ground black pepper
1 soft lettuce, shredded

*Decoration*
Sprigs of parsley
Wedges of lemon

1. Mix the eggs and white crab meat together in a bowl.
2. Combine all the remaining ingredients, except the lettuce, in a separate bowl and pour over the egg and crab mixture. Mix well.
3. Fill 24 goblets with the shredded lettuce and top with the crab cocktail mixture. Garnish with sprigs of parsley and lemon wedges.

# SEAFOOD MOUSSE

This delicious recipe makes an eye-catching item on a cold buffet. It is best made the day before.

**Serves 24**

**675g cod, haddock or other white fish fillet**
**300ml dry white wine**
**Salt and freshly ground black pepper**
**350g peeled prawns**
**475ml tomato juice**
**475ml mayonnaise**
**2 green peppers, seeded and very finely diced**
**4 tbsp lemon juice**
**4 tbsp freshly chopped parsley**
**Pinch of mixed dried herbs**
**50g gelatine powder**
**6 egg whites**

*Decoration*
**Thin lemon slices**
**Prawns in their shells**

1. Fill two 1.2-litre fluted moulds with cold water.
2. Place the fish fillets in a saucepan and add the wine and seasoning. Bring to the boil, reduce the heat and simmer for 5 minutes or so until the fish is cooked through.

3. Remove the fish from the cooking liquor, retaining the latter on one side. Remove any skin or bone from the fish and process in a blender or food processor with the prawns and tomato juice. Mix in the mayonnaise, peppers, lemon juice and herbs.

4. Mix the gelatine with the cooking liquor from the fish and stir over a low heat until completely dissolved. Leave to cool a little and mix into the fish mixture. Correct the seasoning, if necessary.

5. Whisk the egg whites until they are very stiff and add a tablespoonful to the mixture. Fold in the rest of the egg whites.

6. Tip the water from the moulds, and spoon in the fish mixture. Place in the fridge to set. To unmould quickly, dip the mould in hot water and immediately turn out the mousse.

7. Decorate with very thin slices of lemon and prawns in their shells.

# PORK AND HERB TERRINE

For the best results make this party terrine the day before you want to serve it. It does not need to be weighted down, but it does need to settle overnight to make it easier to slice. Don't be put off by the long list of ingredients as it is quite easy to make.

**Serves 20**

450g lean pork, cubed
1 onion, finely chopped
2 knobs of butter
450g fresh spinach
225g cooked ham, diced
225g streaky bacon, diced
1 clove garlic, peeled and crushed
2 tbsp freshly chopped basil
2 tbsp freshly chopped parsley
2 tbsp freshly chopped chervil
2 spikes fresh rosemary, finely chopped
4 eggs, beaten
Salt and freshly ground black pepper
½ tsp nutmeg
115g chicken livers, diced
3 tbsp double cream
2 tbsp gelatine powder
225g streaky bacon, rind removed and stretched along its
  length with the back of a knife
Sprigs of fresh rosemary, for decoration

1. Preheat the oven to 160°C/325°F/Gas 3.
2. Mince the pork in a food processor. Fry the onion in one knob of butter until transparent. Add the spinach and continue to cook until the spinach has wilted.
3. Chop coarsely and mix with the pork. Process again. Stir in the diced ham, bacon, garlic, herbs, eggs, seasoning and nutmeg.
4. Fry the chicken livers in the second knob of butter until golden. Stir in the cream, and the gelatine dissolved in a spoonful of hot water. Add to the terrine mixture.
5. Line a 1.25–1.5kg terrine dish or tin with the bacon. Spoon in the terrine mixture and cook for 2 hours. Remove from the oven and pour out any excess liquid. Leave to cool and then chill overnight in the fridge.
6. Decorate with sprigs of fresh rosemary. To serve, slice into 10 and then cut each slice in half.

# SUN-DRIED TOMATO AND GOATS' CHEESE TART

Long tarts like this one slice well and fit on the buffet table rather better than round tarts. Double up the quantities to make two or four tarts depending on the number of guests.

**Serves 15-16**

225g shortcrust pastry
Plain flour, for rolling out
1 small goats' cheese log, sliced
6 pieces of sun-dried tomato, soaked in water, drained and
  chopped
100g grated Parmesan cheese
4 eggs, beaten
150ml single cream
150ml milk
Salt and freshly ground black pepper

1. Roll out the pastry on a floured surface/board and use to line a 31 x 23cm Swiss roll tin. Prick the base with a fork and line with foil over the pastry. Fill with dried beans or lentils and bake at 190°C/375°F/Gas 5 for 10 minutes. Remove the beans and foil from the tart and return to the oven for a further 5 minutes.

2. Arrange the slices of goats' cheese over the base of the tart and sprinkle with sun-dried tomatoes and Parmesan cheese. Mix the remaining ingredients in a jug and pour evenly over the tart. Return to the oven and bake for 50–55 minutes until golden on top and set in the centre.

3. Serve hot or cold, cut into small squares.

## VARIATIONS

In place of sun-dried tomatoes and goats' cheese try:

- Crumbled blue cheese and cooked leeks
- Roasted peppers with pecorino cheese mixed with ricotta
- Asparagus spears with mascarpone cheese

# CORONATION CHICKEN

This is an ever-popular buffet dish; people simply do not seem to tire of it. It is quite quick and easy to make on the day.

**Serves 25**

**3 x 2kg roasting chickens**
**50g butter**
**Salt and freshly ground black pepper**
**3 onions, finely chopped**
**1 clove garlic, peeled and chopped**
**3 tbsp olive oil**
**3–4 tbsp curry powder**
**450ml mayonnaise**
**15ml soured cream or yoghurt**

*Decoration*
**Sprigs of watercress**
**Mango chutney**

1. Rub the chickens with butter and season. Roast at 200°C/400°F/Gas 6 for 1¼ hours. Leave to cool.
2. Fry the onions and garlic in the olive oil for 3–4 minutes to soften, but do not brown. Stir in the curry powder and cook for a further 2 minutes, Leave to cool.
3. Remove all the chicken meat from the skin and bones and cut into large chunks. Mix the mayonnaise and soured cream or yoghurt with the curry mixture and fold in the chicken meat.
4. Spoon onto a serving plate and garnish with sprigs of watercress and spoonfuls of mango chutney.

# GRAPE AND PAPRIKA CHICKEN

This velvety variation on Coronation Chicken looks very pretty when served with Spring Vegetable Salad (page 202) or Fruity Rice Salad (page 209). It is relatively easy to scale up for larger quantities when you might consider using whole chickens for a more economical dish.

**Serves 20-24**

2 large onions, sliced
2 cloves garlic, peeled and crushed
2 tbsp olive oil
300ml carton plain yoghurt
20ml chicken stock
4 tbsp mild paprika
Salt
12 chicken breast fillets, cubed
450g green grapes, halved and stoned
350ml mayonnaise
Sprigs of fresh herbs, for decoration, such as dill or chervil

1. Gently fry the onion and garlic in the oil for 2–3 minutes. Add the yoghurt, stock, paprika and salt and stir well. Next, add the chicken and bring to the boil. Simmer gently for 45 minutes.
2. The mixture should be fairly dry by the end of the cooking time. Leave to cool. When cold, stir in half of the grapes and the mayonnaise. Spoon onto a serving plate. Garnish with the rest of the grapes and sprigs of fresh herbs.

# CHEESE LOG

This is a very versatile dish, which you can make with a variety of different cheeses such as Cheddar, Lancashire and Cheshire. You can also change the vegetable base and use grated carrots or turnips in place of the celeriac.

**Serves 20**

**675g red Leicester cheese, grated**
**350g celeriac, peeled and grated**
**6 tbsp freshly chopped parsley**
**6 tbsp dry-roasted peanuts, coarsely chopped**
**100ml mayonnaise**
**Salt and freshly ground black pepper**
**1 large bunch parsley, chopped**

*Decoration*
**Cherry tomatoes**
**Sprigs of continental parsley**

1. Mix the cheese with the celeriac, parsley, dry-roasted nuts and mayonnaise and season to taste. Spoon the mixture down the centre of a large rectangle of baking parchment and roll up into a log shape, about 36cm in length.
2. Chill in the fridge for 1 hour. Carefully remove the paper from the log and roll in chopped parsley.
3. Serve on a long serving dish on its own or in a pair. Cut into slices with a sharp knife. Decorate with cherry tomatoes and sprigs of parsley.

# OLD-FASHIONED EGG FLAN

This simple sounding and easy-to-make dish looks great on a buffet and is always a knockout. Make plenty as guests will come back for more!

**Serves 10–12**

**1 x 400g packet frozen shortcrust pastry, thawed**
**Plain flour, for rolling out**
**9 eggs, beaten**
**100ml milk**
**Salt and freshly ground black pepper**
**25g butter**

*Garnish*
**6 small tomatoes, peeled and thinly sliced**
**17g fresh or frozen peas, cooked with mint**
**Sprigs of fresh mint (optional)**

1. Preheat the oven to 200°C/400°F/Gas 6.
2. Roll out the pastry on a floured surface/board until it is fairly thin and use to line a 28cm loose-based flan tin. Prick the base with a fork and line the flan with a round of baking parchment. Cover the base with baking beans and bake for 20 minutes. Remove the beans and paper and continue baking for a further 5–10 minutes until the flan case is fully cooked. Remove from the oven and leave to cool.
3. Meanwhile, beat the eggs with the milk and seasoning. Melt the butter in a non-stick saucepan. Add the egg mixture and scramble the eggs, beating all the time with a wooden spoon. When the eggs are almost cooked, remove from the heat and continue to beat with the wooden spoon. The eggs should be quite creamy. Leave to cool, stirring from time to time.
4. Just before the flan is to be served, spoon the cold scrambled eggs into the pastry base and spread evenly.
5. Decorate the top with rings of sliced tomatoes and peas. Finish off with a few sprigs of fresh mint, if desired. Cut into wedges to serve.

# CREAMY FISH PIE
# WITH SCALLOPED POTATOES

The fresh herbs in this deliciously creamy dish give a wonderful flavour to this classic fish pie. The dish can be prepared in advance to the stage just before the potatoes are added and it goes into the oven. Cover with cling film and keep in the fridge. Half an hour before you need to cook it, remove from the fridge and allow to warm up at room temperature before adding the potatoes and baking in the oven.

**Serves 24**

3kg cod fillet, skinned
2kg monkfish, boned and skinned
About 1–1½ litres milk
Salt and freshly ground black pepper
½ tsp ground mace or grated nutmeg
1 litre double cream
2kg potatoes, peeled and sliced
500g peeled prawns
250g butter
300g plain flour
Large bunch parsley, freshly chopped
100g butter, melted

1. Preheat the oven to 200°C/400°F/Gas 6.

2. Place the fish in a pan and barely cover with milk. Add the seasoning and mace or nutmeg. Bring to the boil and simmer very gently for 10 minutes or until the fish is cooked. Drain the liquid off into a measuring jug. Add the cream and make up to 2 litres with more milk, if necessary. Keep on one side.

3. Cook the potatoes in plenty of boiling, salted water for about 10 minutes until almost tender. Drain and keep on one side.

4. Cut the fish into bite-sized pieces and mix with the prawns.

5. Melt the butter in a pan with the flour. Stir in the milk and cream mixture and bring to the boil, stirring all the time until the sauce thickens. Add the fish and the parsley and remove from the heat. Correct the seasoning, if necessary.

6. Spoon into a large shallow dish. Arrange the potatoes in two overlapping rings round the dish, leaving the centre free. Brush the potatoes with the melted butter and cook for 35 minutes. Brown under the grill, if necessary.

# CHICKEN AND HAM LATTICE PIE

This pie looks very attractive on the buffet table so, if you can, leave cutting it into slices until after the guests come to the buffet table.

**Serves 24**

1kg shortcrust pastry
Plain flour, for rolling out
675g cooked chicken
400g cooked ham
80g thyme and onion, or sage and bacon stuffing mix
4 eggs, beaten
½ tsp grated nutmeg
2 tbsp freshly chopped parsley
2 tbsp freshly chopped chives

1. Preheat the oven to 180°C/350°F/Gas 4.
2. Roll out the pastry on a floured surface/board and use two-thirds to line two long rectangular loose-based flan tins, about 27.5 x 10cm, retaining the trimmings.
3. Mince or finely chop half the chicken and ham. Cut the remaining meat into pieces. Make up the stuffing mix by pouring on 2 teaspoons boiling water and leave to stand for 10 minutes.
4. Stir all the meat, three-quarters of the beaten egg, the nutmeg and the fresh herbs into the stuffing mixture.
5. Spoon into the pastry and spread smoothly. Cut the remaining pastry into thin strips and use to make a latticework pattern over the flan. Brush with the remaining beaten egg. Bake for 40–45 minutes until the pastry is crisp and golden. Serve hot or cold.

# SAUSAGE AND CREAM CHEESE PIE

This unusual but economical pie looks good on the buffet table. Buy good-quality sausage meat, preferably from a butcher who makes his own. The pie is best served hot.

**Serves 28-30**

900g pork sausage meat
1 tsp dried oregano or mixed herbs
Salt and freshly ground black pepper
350g cream cheese
2 tbsp tomato purée
900g frozen puff pastry, thawed
Plain flour, for rolling out
1 egg, beaten

1. Preheat the oven to 190°C/375°F/Gas 5.
2. Mix the sausage meat with the herbs and seasoning. Divide into two portions and keep on one side.
3. Mix together the cream cheese and tomato purée.
4. Next, divide the pastry roughly into two 240g and two 210g portions. Roll out the two smaller portions on a floured surface/board to make two rectangles approximately 30 x 12cm and place on baking trays.
5. Spread one portion of sausage meat over each piece of pastry, leaving about 1cm around the edges. Top with the cream cheese mixture. Roll out the remaining pieces of pastry to about 32 x 15cm and use to cover the pies.
6. Seal the edges with a little water and pinch well together. Brush with beaten egg and prick the top of each pie with a fork. Bake for 30–35 minutes until golden brown and well risen.
7. Cut into slices to serve.

# DECORATIVE CHARCUTERIE PLATTER

The secret of this plate is to arrange the meats as attractively as possible in geometric patterns. Fold the slices or make into rolls or fan shapes for extra interest.

**Serves 20**

250g cooked ham, sliced
1 x 300g tin white asparagus tips
250g air-dried Parma, Serrano or Westphalian ham, sliced
175g salami, sliced
100g chorizo, sliced
100g kassler or smoked pork, sliced
250g small size mortadella, sliced
250g brawn sausage

*Garnish*
1 egg, hard-boiled and sliced
Broad-leaf parsley
3 tomato skin flowers (see Tip opposite)

1. Cut the slices of ham in half and roll each one round an asparagus tip. Arrange these asparagus rolls at one end of a large oval platter.
2. Fold the air-dried ham into rolls and arrange half of them down the centre of the platter from the asparagus rolls.
3. Make the salami and chorizo slices into funnels by folding them twice. Arrange on each side of the air-dried ham rolls.

4. Next, add a roll of kassler or smoked pork on one side and the remaining air-dried ham rolls on the other.
5. Fold the mortadella and the brawn sausage in half and arrange in rows on the outside.
6. Decorate with sliced hard-boiled egg, parsley and tomato skin flowers.

**TIP**
Carefully peel the tomatoes with a sharp knife to make a long piece of skin about 1cm wide. Roll this around itself to form a flower shape.

# ROAST GAMMON WITH REDCURRANT GLAZE AND CLOVES

This easy-to-cook and easy-to-carve joint is ideal for the cold buffet table.

**Serves 20**

**2 x 2.5kg prime roast gammon joints**
**3–4 tbsp redcurrant jelly**
**75g whole cloves**
**Sprigs of watercress, for garnish**

1. Preheat the oven to 190°C/375°F/Gas 5.
2. Remove the joints from their bags and wrap each one in foil. Roast for 2½ hours. Remove the foil and the retaining netting. Leave to cool.
3. Cut off any excess fat. Spread each joint all over with redcurrant jelly and stud with cloves. Return to the oven and cook for a further 20 minutes.
4. Garnish with sprigs of watercress.

# MIXED-LEAF SALAD WITH VINAIGRETTE

Beware of preparing too much salad. People do not take as much salad from a buffet table as they might eat in other circumstances.

**Serves 24**

**750–800g colourful mixed salad leaves**

*Vinaigrette*
**150ml olive oil**
**50ml good red wine vinegar**
**Salt and freshly ground black pepper**
**A little French mustard (optional)**

1. Wash and drain the salad leaves really well and dry on kitchen paper. Place in a large bowl, or two smaller bowls if there are to be two lines to the buffet table. Cover the bowls with cling film and store in the fridge until required.
2. Blend the vinaigrette ingredients with a wire whisk and pour over the salads at the last minute. Toss and serve.

# CARROT SLAW

You can easily buy ready-made coleslaw if time is tight, but home-made, as usual, has a much better flavour.

**Serves 25–30**

1 small white cabbage, very finely shredded
900g large carrots, coarsely grated
2 tbsp lemon juice
4 tbsp flaked almonds
4 tbsp raisins or sultanas
125ml mayonnaise
A little ready-made mustard (optional)
Salt and freshly ground black pepper

1. Place the two prepared vegetables in a large bowl and toss with the lemon juice.
2. Add all the remaining ingredients and mix well together.
3. Spoon into a serving bowl and serve at once or cover with cling film and keep in the fridge until required.

# WALDORF SALAD

This American salad is another buffet favourite.

**Serves 20-24**

**400g celery sticks**
**4 large apples, cored and peeled**
**200g chopped walnuts**
**250ml mayonnaise**
**3 tbsp lemon juice**
**Salt and freshly ground black pepper**

1. Cut the celery sticks and apples into small dice. Stir in the chopped walnuts and then the mayonnaise and lemon juice.
2. Season to taste and chill for a short while before serving.

# RUSSIAN SALAD

This is another salad that is always popular. Serve it on a cold buffet or use as part of a plated first course with hard-boiled eggs and flaked tuna, or with salami triangles, olives and rocket.

**Serves 20-24**

**400g carrots, peeled and cut into thick batons**
**650g potatoes, peeled and cut into quarters**
**150g peas**
**250g mayonnaise, plus extra for serving**
**50ml lemon juice**
**Salt and freshly ground black pepper**

1. Place the carrots in the base of a pan and cover with water. Add a steamer containing the potatoes and cover with a lid. Bring to the boil and cook for 12 minutes until the vegetables are almost cooked.
2. Add the peas to the carrots and continue cooking for a few minutes until the peas are cooked. Remove all the vegetables from the pan and leave to cool.
3. Dice the potatoes and carrots and mix with peas.
4. Stir the lemon juice into the mayonnaise in a large bowl and fold the vegetables into the mixture. Season to taste and chill. Just before serving, fluff up with a fork and add a little more mayonnaise.

# CORIANDER AND CHERVIL POTATOES

Crunchy coriander seeds give a lightly orangey flavour to the potatoes. Freshly chopped herbs can be used in the same way to give a range of different potato salads.

**Serves 24**

**2.25kg new potatoes**
**Salt**
**4 tbsp whole coriander seeds**
**250ml extra virgin olive oil**
**2 tbsp red wine vinegar**
**8 tbsp freshly chopped chervil**
**Freshly ground black pepper**
**Sprig of chervil, for decoration**

1. Scrub the potatoes and boil in salted water for 10–15 minutes then, depending on size, cut into halves.
2. Toast the coriander seeds under the grill, cool and crush, and mix with the potatoes.
3. Mix together the olive oil, vinegar, chervil and pepper, pour over the potatoes and toss well. Serve hot or cold, garnished with chervil.

# MEDITERRANEAN ROASTED VEGETABLE SALAD

This colourful salad looks great on the buffet table. For a more substantial dish, stir in 6 tablespoons cooked couscous.

**Serves 20**

**4 large red peppers, seeded and cut into four**
**2 large aubergines, sliced**
**4 courgettes, cut into thick slices**
**Extra virgin olive oil**
**24 cherry tomatoes**
**1 bunch rocket**
**2 handfuls baby spinach leaves**
**24 stoned Greek black olives, for garnish**

1. Spread the prepared vegetables (not the tomatoes) over two or three baking trays and drizzle with extra virgin olive oil.
2. Bake at 180°C/350°F/Gas 4 for about half an hour or until the vegetables start to brown just a little. Halfway through, turn the slices over and drizzle with a little more olive oil. Remove from the oven and leave to cool.
3. Bake the cherry tomatoes in the same way on a separate tray, allowing about 15 minutes cooking time. Leave to cool.
4. Wash and dry the rocket and spinach leaves and place in a large bowl with half the baked vegetables. Spoon into two large entrée dishes and top with the rest of the vegetables. Dot with black olives and drizzle more extra virgin olive oil over the top.

# MUSHROOM AND SWEETCORN SALAD

Raw mushrooms are delicious in salads. They do not need to be peeled. Simply wipe and dry and trim off the end of the stalks.

**Serves 15-20**

4 large dessert apples
2 tbsp lemon juice
450g cooked or canned sweetcorn kernels
450g button mushrooms, wiped and sliced
1 small head celery, very finely chopped
4 tbsp olive oil
Salt and freshly ground black pepper
Pinch of dried thyme
Lettuce leaves, torn in smaller pieces

1. Core and chop the apples and drop into the lemon juice. Add all the remaining ingredients, except the lettuce leaves, and toss well together. Cover with cling film and store in the fridge until required.
2. To serve, line a salad bowl with the lettuce and spoon on the apple, mushroom and sweetcorn mixture.

# SPRING VEGETABLE SALAD

This unusual salad is very popular and makes a real change from lettuce- and tomato-based salads. For the best results, cook the vegetables very lightly until they are just, but only just, tender and toss in the dressing while still hot.

**Serves 20**

675g baby carrots, trimmed and scraped
Salt
3 bunches bulbous spring onions, trimmed
350g small green beans, topped and tailed
175g fresh or frozen peas

*Dressing*
100ml olive oil
3 tbsp lemon juice
2 tsp Dijon mustard
Salt and freshly ground black pepper

1. Place the carrots in a pan with plenty of salted water and bring to the boil. After 5 minutes, add the spring onions and continue cooking for about 8–10 minutes until just tender.
2. Place the beans in another pan and cover with water. Cook for 5–6 minutes and add the peas; continue cooking for a further 2 minutes. Fresh peas may need to be added a little earlier to cook through.
3. Mix all the dressing ingredients together with a fork or shake in a small jar. Drain the vegetables and pour the dressing over the top. Leave to cool and chill for ½ hour before serving.

# FUSILLI WITH PRAWN AND HERB SAUCE

This is a quick dish to make and it can be prepared at the very last minute.

**Serves 20**

1.5kg fusilli
Salt
1.5kg Boursin or tartar herb and garlic cheese (10 packs)
600ml white wine
1kg frozen peeled prawns

1. Cook the fusilli in a large pan of boiling salted water for about 10–12 minutes, as stated on the pack, until al dente.
2. Heat the herb and garlic cheese in a large saucepan, stirring in the white wine as it heats up and taking care not to overcook. Stir in the prawns at the last minute.
3. When the pasta is cooked, drain well and toss with the hot sauce.

# BUTTONS AND BOWS PASTA (FARFALLE)

For the best results, keep the meatballs fairly small so that they do not dwarf the pasta shapes.

**Serves 25-30**

1.5g lamb, minced
2 tbsp freshly chopped mint
4 tbsp freshly chopped parsley
1 tsp chilli or cayenne powder
Salt and freshly ground black pepper
4 tbsp olive oil
4 cloves garlic, peeled and crushed
4 x 400g tins chopped tomatoes, drained
1.5kg pasta in the shape of bows (farfalle)
Sprigs of mint, for garnish

1. Mix the lamb with the mint, parsley, chilli or cayenne powder and salt and pepper. Shape into tiny balls.
2. Heat half the olive oil in a frying pan over a high heat. Add the meatballs in batches and fry until browned. Reduce the heat and continue to fry for a further 2–3 minutes.
3. In a saucepan, mix together the garlic, tomatoes and the remaining olive oil and simmer gently for 15 minutes.
4. Cook and drain the pasta as stated on the pack. Toss the pasta with the tomato sauce and carefully stir in the meatballs.
5. Serve garnished with sprigs of mint.

# RAINBOW PASTA SALAD

Look for packets of three-flavour pasta spirals for a really colourful effect.

**Serves 20**

**450g mixed plain, tomato and spinach pasta spirals**
**Salt**
**4 tbsp olive oil**
**1 tbsp red wine vinegar**
**1 bunch spring onions, very finely chopped**
**18–20 black olives**

1. Cook the pasta spirals in plenty of boiling salted water, as directed on the pack. When they are just tender to the bite, or *al dente*, drain very well.
2. Toss in the oil and vinegar and leave to cool.
3. Add the spring onions and black olives and toss again.

# SPINACH, RICOTTA
# AND FETA LASAGNE

The four main components of this dish can be prepared in advance and then reheated and put together to cook just before serving. If you are serving the dish as part of a pasta buffet allow for about two-thirds of the guests to choose this dish and the same for the two previous hot pasta dishes. If you make all three dishes for everyone you will be left with quite a lot of leftovers.

**Serves 12–14**

**1kg frozen leaf spinach**
**2 tbsp olive oil**
**2 large onions, finely chopped**
**2 cloves garlic, peeled and finely chopped**
**Salt and freshly ground black pepper**
**600g ricotta cheese**
**200g feta cheese**
**3 tbsp freshly chopped parsley**
**75g butter**
**75g plain flour**
**350ml milk**
**150ml white wine**
**12 sheets lasagne (approx. 17 x 8cm)**
**50g Parmesan cheese**

1. Thaw the spinach over a low heat and then cook for about 5–8 minutes until tender. Drain well.

2. Meanwhile, heat the olive oil in a large pan and fry the onions and garlic until lightly browned. Stir in the cooked spinach and season to taste. Keep on one side.

3. Mix the ricotta and feta cheeses together in a bowl, stir in the parsley and season.

4. Melt the butter in a saucepan and stir in the flour. Gradually add the milk and wine and bring to the boil. Season and cook gently for about 3 minutes. The sauce should have the consistency of cream; it should not be too thick. Remove from the heat and cover with cling film to stop the sauce forming a skin. Keep on one side.

5. Cook the lasagne in plenty of boiling water for 3–4 minutes. Drain and leave in cold water if not using straight away.

6. To make up the lasagne, preheat the oven to 180°C/350°F/Gas 4. Reheat the spinach and white sauce, adding a little more milk to the latter if it is too thick.

7. Place a quarter of the white sauce in the base of two square tray-bake tins (bases 18 x18cm) or one large roasting tin. Top with a third of the spinach mix and then a third of the mixed cheeses. Arrange two sheets of lasagne on top. Repeat these layers twice more.

8. Spread the final quarter of white sauce over the top and sprinkle with the Parmesan cheese. Bake for 30–35 minutes.

# ROSY RICE SALAD

If you are in a hurry, this pretty dish can be made with plain uncoloured rice alone, but the end result will not be quite as effective. You can use the beetroot to make a soup with cabbage another day.

**Serves 35**

3 cooked beetroot, finely chopped
1.75 litres hot water
1kg long-grain rice
225g peeled prawns
225g smoked ham, very finely chopped
2 small red peppers, seeded and finely chopped
350g sweetcorn kernels
60ml extra virgin olive oil
1 tbsp cider or wine vinegar
Salt and freshly ground black pepper
Sprigs of parsley, for decoration

1. Place the beetroot in a bowl and pour half the water over the top. Leave to stand for 1 hour.
2. Drain the liquid into a pan and discard the beetroot. Add half the rice and bring to the boil. Cover with a lid, reduce the heat and simmer for 15–20 minutes, until all the liquid has been absorbed and the rice is tender. Leave to cool.
3. Cook the remaining rice and plain water in the same way and leave to cool.
4. Mix the two batches of rice together and then add all the remaining ingredients. Toss well and spoon into a serving bowl. Garnish with sprigs of parsley.

# FRUITY RICE SALAD

The fruit gives a really fresh taste and crunchy texture to this unusual rice salad.

**Serves 15–20**

600ml orange juice
300ml water
Salt and freshly ground black pepper
450g long-grain rice
4 tbsp extra virgin olive oil
1 tbsp lemon juice
2 firm bananas, diced
2 red-skinned apples, cored and diced
2 green-skinned apples, cored and diced
4 tbsp raisins or sultanas
1 bunch spring onions, very finely chopped
4 tbsp freshly chopped parsley

1. Mix the orange juice and water in a large saucepan and bring to the boil. Add 1 teaspoon salt and the rice and return to the boil. Stir once, cover with a lid and simmer for 15–16 minutes until all the liquid has been absorbed and the rice is cooked.
2. Fluff up with a fork and leave to cool. When the rice is lukewarm, stir in the oil and lemon juice and leave to cool completely.
3. Mix in all the remaining ingredients just before serving and check the seasoning.

# PINEAPPLE AND ORANGE STARS

This very attractive-looking dessert is simplicity itself. Prepare in advance and keep in the fridge.

**Serves 12**

**1 large fresh pineapple, cut into 12 rings and trimmed, or
  3 x 225g tins pineapple slices, drained
2 kiwifruit, peeled and cut into 12 slices
4 small oranges, peeled and segmented
75ml double cream, whipped
3–4 large fresh strawberries, sliced**

1. Place the pineapple rings on one large serving plate. Top with a slice of kiwifruit.
2. Remove any pith or tough membranes from the orange segments and arrange in a star-shape around the kiwi on each slice of pineapple.
3. Pipe a rosette of cream in the centre of each one and top with a slice of strawberry.

# FRESH STRAWBERRY CHEESECAKE

Cheesecakes are sometimes seen as rather old-fashioned but they are quick and easy to make and disappear from the buffet table rather fast!

**Serves 12**

1 packet sweet biscuits, crushed
75g butter, melted
50g sugar
450g strawberries
350g cottage cheese
Juice of 1 lemon
150ml soured cream
1 x 12g sachet powdered gelatine
300ml orange juice

1. Preheat the oven to 140°C/275°F/Gas 1.
2. Mix the biscuits with the butter and sugar and press into the base of a 27.5cm loose-based cake tin. Bake for 8 minutes and leave to cool.
3. Sieve 175g of the strawberries with the cottage cheese, then mix with the lemon juice and soured cream or process in a food processor.
4. Mix the gelatine with 3 tablespoons of the orange juice in a cup and place in a pan of hot water to dissolve. Stir into the strawberry cheese mixture with the rest of the orange juice. Pour over the baked base and place in the fridge to set.
5. Slice the rest of the strawberries and arrange in a decorative pattern on top of the cheesecake. Cut into wedges to serve.

## VARIATIONS

Almost any kind of soft fruits can be used in this way. Try with the same weight of ripe raspberries or blueberries.

# SUMMER FRUIT PLATTER

Almost any fruit in season can be used on this wonderful buffet centrepiece. The secret lies in the attractive arrangement of the fruit on a glass mirror.

**Serves 20**

**2 pineapples, cored and sliced lengthways into wedges**
**2 large or 4 small melons, seeded and cut into thin wedges**
**8 kiwifruit, peeled and sliced**
**450g mixed raspberries and blackberries**

1. Arrange the pineapple and melon wedges along the sides of an oval or rectangular mirror.
2. Place the kiwi slices in a semi-circle at one end and fill the centre with the soft fruits.

## OTHER GOOD FRUIT COMBINATIONS

**Mixed berries:** strawberries, raspberries, blackberries, and blueberries

**Mixed tropical fruits:** sliced star fruits, mangoes, and pineapple scattered with pomegranate seeds

# NORMANDY APPLE TART

This classic French tart makes a good contrast to a creamy dessert and is relatively easy to make. Serve with a bowl of whipped cream.

**Serves 12**

*Pastry*
**225g plain flour**
**Salt**
**100g sugar**
**100g butter**
**1 egg, beaten**

*Filling*
**1.5kg cooking apples, peeled, cored and sliced**
**4–5 eating apples, peeled, cored and sliced**
**4–5 tbsp apricot jam**
**2 tbsp water**

1. Preheat the oven to 200°C/400°F/Gas 6.
2. Sift the flour into a bowl with the salt and add the sugar and the butter. Rub the fat into the dry ingredients until the mixture resembles fine breadcrumbs. Stir in the egg a little at a time and mix to a stiff dough with your fingers; if necessary, add a little water.
3. Press into a 27.5cm flan tin, working the pastry across the base and up the sides. Leave to stand.
4. To make the filling, cook the cooking apples in 1 tablespoon water until they are soft. Mash well with a fork or sieve and leave to cool.
5. Spread the cooled apple over the pastry base. Arrange the sliced eating apples over the top. Melt the jam with a little water and brush over the top layer of apples.
6. Bake for 30 minutes. Reduce the heat to 190°C/375°F/Gas 5 and then continue cooking until the pastry is crisp and the top of the flan is well browned.

# TIPSY TRIFLE

This classic trifle is everyone's favourite dessert. It's made with custard powder enriched with egg yolks. If the budget is really tight, you could use another tablespoon or so of custard powder in place of one of the egg yolks, but the end result is not nearly so good.

**Serves 10-12**

1 box trifle sponges
4 tbsp raspberry jam
2 tbsp caster sugar
4 tbsp warm water
100ml brandy or sherry
3 tbsp custard powder
600ml milk
2 egg yolks
25g caster sugar
Few drops vanilla essence
225ml whipping cream

*Decoration*
Toasted flaked almonds
4–5 glacé cherries, quartered

1. Cut the sponges in half and spread with jam. Place in the base of a glass dish.
2. Dissolve the sugar in the warm water, mix with the brandy or sherry and pour over the sponges.
3. Mix the custard powder with 4 tablespoons milk and beat in the egg yolks, sugar and vanilla essence in a bowl. Heat the rest of the milk in a pan to just below boiling and pour over the custard mixture. Return to the pan and bring back just to the boil, stirring all the time. Cook gently for 2–3 minutes until thickened.
4. Leave to cool a little and then pour over the sponges. Leave to cool completely.
5. Whisk the cream and pipe over the top of the trifle. Decorate with toasted flaked almonds and glacé cherries.

## VARIATIONS

A layer of fruit adds interest and helps the trifle to serve even more people. Try one of the following ideas:

- 1kg cooking apples, cooked, puréed and chilled with Calvados in place of the brandy or sherry.
- 1 x 600g tin fruit cocktail, drained.
- 4 sliced bananas, tossed in lemon juice and rum in place of brandy or sherry.

# YORKSHIRE CURD TARTS

Some recipes for these traditional tarts use just saffron and no raisins, and others use raisins and nutmeg or grated orange rind – take your pick.

**Makes 24**

75g curd cheese or a fairly dry soft cheese
75g Wensleydale cheese, grated
3 eggs, beaten
2 tbsp double cream
75g raisins
1 tsp grated nutmeg, orange rind or powdered saffron
1 x 450g packet shortcrust pastry
Plain flour, for rolling out

1. Preheat the oven to 190°C/375°F/Gas 5 and grease a bun-tray.
2. Beat the curd cheese with the Wensleydale, eggs and cream and stir in the raisins and your chosen flavouring.
3. Roll out the pastry on a floured surface/board and use to line 24 bun or tart tins. Fill with the cheese mixture and bake for 20–25 minutes until set and lightly browned.

# BANANA AND ORANGE CHARLOTTE

Best made the day before, this very effective-looking dessert is quite easy to make. For larger numbers simply make two or three.

**Serves 8-10**

**2 packets orange jelly, broken into pieces**
**5 large bananas**
**24–26 sponge fingers or Boudoir biscuits**
**Juice of ½ lemon**
**450ml double cream**

1. Dissolve the jelly in 150ml boiling water. Add another 300ml cold water and stir well. Spoon a thin layer of the jelly into the base of an 18cm round, deep cake tin. Chill in the fridge until set.
2. When set, peel one of the bananas and cut into thin rounds. Arrange in a circle along the edge of the jelly. Cover with another layer of jelly and return to the fridge to set.
3. Trim the sides of the sponge fingers so that they will fit closely together and stand them, sugared sides towards the tin, all the way around the walls of the tin.
4. Peel the remaining bananas and mash with the lemon juice. Whisk the cream until thick and add the remaining jelly, which should be almost set. Fold in the mashed banana and spoon into the prepared tin.
5. Place in the fridge to set. Just before serving, trim the sponge fingers to the level of the filling. Dip the base quickly in hot water to loosen it, invert on to a serving dish and lift the tin away. Decorate by tying a pretty ribbon all the way round the outside.

# STRAWBERRY FEATHER CAKE

This feather-light, fatless sponge, filled with liqueur, cream and strawberries, makes a lovely cake for a summer wedding. The cake also freezes well unfilled and so can be prepared in advance.

**Serves 10**

4 eggs
100g caster sugar
Pinch of salt
100g plain flour

*Filling*
450ml double cream
75g caster sugar
3 tbsp kirsch or Cointreau
100g strawberries, chopped
2 kiwifruit, chopped

*Decoration*
1 kiwifruit, sliced
2–3 strawberries, chopped

1. Preheat the oven to 190°C/375°F/Gas 5 and grease and flour two 20cm sandwich tins.
2. Whisk the eggs, sugar and salt until thick and creamy and light in colour. This will take 7–10 minutes by hand and a much shorter time in a good processor. Fold in the flour and spoon into the prepared cake tins.
3. Bake for 25 minutes. Cool on a wire rack.
4. To make the filling, whisk 300ml of the cream with the sugar and liqueur and mix with the chopped strawberries and kiwifruit. Spread half over one cake and top with the second cake. Pipe the remaining cream around the top of the cake and arrange the sliced kiwifruit and chopped strawberries in the centre.

# ORANGE CASSATA BOMBE

This dessert can be made well in advance and simply stored in the freezer. Remember to remove it from the freezer about 15 minutes before serving or it may be very hard.

**Serves 12**

2½ tbsp caster sugar
100ml water
3 egg yolks, lightly beaten
350ml whipping cream
3–4 drops vanilla essence
2½ tbsp water
100g plain chocolate, melted
Grated rind of 1 large orange
50g glacé cherries, chopped
25g crystallised ginger, chopped
2 tbsp raisins, chopped
2 tbsp pistachio nuts, chopped

1. Dissolve the sugar in the water over a low heat. As soon as it has all dissolved turn up the heat and boil for 4–5 minutes or until a sugar thermometer registers 101°C/213.8°F. Take the pan off the heat and wait 30 seconds, then pour the syrup in a thin stream onto the egg yolks in a bowl, whisking all the time. Whisk over cold water or ice cubes until the mixture pales, thickens and cools.

2. Whisk the cream lightly with the vanilla essence and fold into the egg mixture.

3. Divide the mixture into two-thirds and one-third portions. To the larger quantity, stir in the melted chocolate and then chill for about 1½ hours until firm. Use this mixture to line a 600ml bombe mould or pudding basin. Place in the freezer and leave to set.

4. Fold the grated orange rind, cherries, ginger, raisins and nuts into the remaining third of the ice-cream mixture. Spoon this into the centre of the set bombe and return to the freezer for 4–6 hours to complete the freezing process.

5. Remove from the freezer 10–15 minutes before cutting into wedge-shaped slices to serve.

# RASPBERRY SHORTCAKES

These little biscuits can be served without the filling with other desserts such as Tia Maria Creams (page 253).

**Makes 28**

400g butter, softened
200g caster sugar
400g plain flour, plus a little extra for rolling out
100g cornflour
100g ground almonds
8 tbsp cocoa powder
1.2 litres double cream
Sifted icing sugar
750g raspberries

1. Preheat the oven to 180°C/350°F/Gas 4 and oil some flat baking sheets.
2. Place the butter and sugar in a food processor and blend until fluffy. Add all the dry ingredients and process until well blended; the mixture should form a stiffish dough. You may need to do this in two or three batches, depending on the capacity of your food processor.
3. Knead each batch of dough lightly and roll out on a floured surface/board to about 5mm thick. Cut into 18 or more squares of about 6cm using a fluted cutter. Transfer to the oiled baking trays and bake for about 15–20 minutes until lightly browned. Repeat until all the dough has been used up and you have 56 shortcake biscuits. Cool on a wire rack.
4. Whip the cream and mix with a little icing sugar. Pipe the cream onto half the squares and then top with the raspberries and the remaining squares. Dust with icing sugar.

# SIT-DOWN MEALS

A full sit-down meal is very hard work for the home-caterer. Ideally, the cook should not be one of the guests, but very often this is not possible. On the other hand, a small sit-down lunch or dinner at home for a wedding or anniversary can be a very intimate and enjoyable family affair.

The best approach is to keep things as simple as possible. Choose food that can be prepared in advance or which does not need very much preparation. Poached Salmon (see pages 170–1), roasts and casseroles all work well. Serve a cold starter and a simple fruit dessert. In this way you will spend the minimum amount of time in the kitchen and the maximum amount with your guests. Alternatively, choose dishes which you can make the day before.

## THE PLAN

Start by looking at the master checklist on pages 5–6. Work through it, adding the relevant sections to your own checklist. Here are some extra points to consider as you go along.

# THE VENUE

Your own home is probably the best venue for a sit-down meal as you will be able to cook in the familiar surroundings of your own kitchen. Next best is to use a friend or relative's house.

Twelve to twenty guests is the range you may be able to cater for at home. Very often the best place to set up the table is the sitting or living room as this is often the largest room in the house. Clear out all the armchairs and improvise a long table, using your own dining table extended with card tables or occasional tables, or hire trestle tables. Another idea is to set up three or four tables for four or six. Chairs can be hired along with the tables.

The same sort of set-up can be arranged in a marquee in the garden, but the cost of a marquee is not usually justifiable for such a small number of guests.

If you are determined to seat 50 or 60, then you will probably have to find an outside venue such as a village hall or sports club. This can work well if there is a kitchen in which to prepare starters and vegetables and to reheat the main course.

# THE SEATING PLAN

The seating plan is one of the most important and at the same time one of the most difficult jobs of a sit-down reception. Who is to sit with whom? The top table is fairly easy. If you are catering for a wedding, the bride and groom, bridesmaids and groomsmen together with the parents will fill the table, with the bride and groom sitting in the centre, parents next and bridesmaids and groomsmen on the outside.

The other tables may be set out as legs to the top table, or they may be large round tables. Either way the most sensible decision is to sit people together who know each other. This will help the party go with a swing and avoid the tedious effort of guests having to talk to people they do not know and with whom they may have nothing in common.

When you have completed the task, make an immediate plan on paper and draw a larger version for display on the day. Place names can be typewritten on cards, or if anyone in the family has a particularly pleasant hand, they look very good written in ink with a fountain pen.

## THE FOOD

The more food you can prepare in advance or buy in the easier it will be for you on the day. Good starters include soups like chilled seafood soup, vichyssoise and gazpacho, prawn cocktail, pâtés and terrines. Most of these can be bought ready-made if you do not have the time or the inclination to make them yourself. Desserts, too, can be bought in. Try your local patisserie for special tarts or meringue-based gateaux. For an even more elaborate meal simply add in a cheese course.

# SIT-DOWN MENU 1

This is a special menu for a small number of people, but it is not too difficult to make for up to 36 people, provided your oven will take three shelves for the Boeuf en Croute.

## MENU

Chilled Seafood Soup (page 237)
Boeuf en Croute (pages 246–7) with peas and potatoes
Passion Fruit Pavlova (page 254)

## PLAN

PREPARE IN ADVANCE
- Cook pavlova base and store in an airtight tin
- Prepare boeuf en croute and leave in the fridge overnight

PREPARE EARLIER IN THE DAY AND COVER IN CLING FILM
- Prepare seafood soup and store in the fridge
- Prepare the vegetables and store in a cool place

AT THE LAST MINUTE
- Cook boeuf en croute
- Cook the vegetables
- Put the pavlova together

# SIT-DOWN MENU 2

This is a vegetarian menu which can be fairly easily prepared for up to about 30 people.

## MENU
Fennel and Avocado Salad (page 239)

Rainbow Roulades (pages 242–3) with minted new potatoes and green beans

Cream-filled Brandy Snaps (pages 258–9) and Meringues (use the recipe for Mini-Meringues, page 149)

## PLAN

### PREPARE IN ADVANCE
- Cook the meringues and store in an airtight tin
- Bake the brandy snaps and store in an airtight tin

### PREPARE EARLIER IN THE DAY AND COVER IN CLING FILM
- Prepare the vegetables
- Prepare ingredients for the roulades and store in a cool place
- Whip the cream for the meringues and brandy snaps and store in the fridge

### AT THE LAST MINUTE
- Prepare fennel and avocado salad
- Prepare and cook rainbow roulades
- Cook the vegetables
- Fill the meringues and brandy snaps with whipped cream

# SIT-DOWN MENU 3

This is a fairly simple menu, which can be prepared for quite large numbers.

## MENU

Pomme D'amour Eggs (page 238)

Beef in Red Wine (pages 250–1) with glazed carrots and new
   potatoes

Sliced Strawberries with Romanoff Cream (page 255)

## PLAN

PREPARE IN ADVANCE

• Prepare and cook the beef in red wine; cool and store in the
  fridge

• Prepare and cook the meringues for the romanoff; store in an
  airtight tin

PREPARE EARLIER IN THE DAY AND COVER IN CLING FILM

• Prepare and finish the pomme d'amour eggs; store in the
  fridge

AT THE LAST MINUTE

• Reheat the beef in red wine, stirring frequently

• Prepare and cook the vegetables

• Finish off the sliced strawberries with romanoff cream

# SIT-DOWN MENU 4

This is a good menu for a summer meal. It is relatively easy to prepare, and one helper in the kitchen to finish off the chicken dish should be sufficient.

## MENU

Italian Stuffed Peppers (page 241)
with crusty French bread or ciabatta
Chicken in Tarragon Cream Sauce (pages 248–9)
with buttered carrots and new potatoes
Lemon Tarts (page 256)
Mixed berry fruit salad

## PLAN

PREPARE EARLIER IN THE DAY AND COVER IN CLING FILM

- Make the individual lemon tarts and store in a cool place
- Prepare the stuffed peppers and store in a cool place
- Prepare the ingredients for the chicken in tarragon cream sauce and store in the fridge
- Make the mixed berry fruit salad and store in the fridge

AT THE LAST MINUTE

- Bake the stuffed peppers
- Cook the chicken in tarragon sauce
- Cook the carrots and new potatoes

# SIT-DOWN MENU 5

This is a traditional menu which is relatively easy to prepare for up to 20 people at Christmas or New Year, or indeed any special family occasion.

## MENU

Smoked Salmon Parcels with Prawns (page 240)

Roast Turkey with Walnut Stuffing (pages 232–3) and Giblet Gravy (page 234)

Fennel in Cream Sauce (page 252)

Roasted potatoes and parsnips

Tia Maria Creams (page 253) with Brandy Snaps (pages 258–9)

Pistachio Nut Fudge (page 257)

## PLAN

PREPARE IN ADVANCE

- Make the pistachio nut fudge
- Make the brandy snaps
- Make the walnut stuffing and giblet gravy

PREPARE EARLIER IN THE DAY AND COVER IN CLING FILM

- Prepare and cook the turkey, timing the bird to be cooked about 15–20 minutes before serving; leave to rest until carving
- Make the smoked salmon parcels with prawns and store in the fridge
- Make the Tia Maria creams and store in the fridge
- Peel and pre-cook the potatoes and parsnips ready for roasting

AT THE LAST MINUTE

- Roast the potatoes and parsnips
- Cook the fennel in cream sauce
- Finish off and carve the turkey
- Finish the giblet gravy

## THE DRINKS

Choose wine to complement the food. Serve a good claret with roasts, a Rioja or an Australian Cabernet or Shiraz with Beef in Red Wine, a Chablis with poached salmon and a Vouvray with poultry dishes.

It is quite a good idea to serve a sparkling wine before the meal. Try a Crémant de Bourgogne or a good Spanish cava. The same wine can be served again for the toasts, or you can switch to champagne.

## THE EQUIPMENT

If you are unable to cobble together a dining table large enough to seat your guests, trestle tables and chairs can be hired from catering-equipment hire companies. You may also need to hire crockery, cutlery and glasses. Check the size of your oven before choosing the menu; will it be big enough to take a large turkey, for example?

## STAFF AND HELPERS

However organised you are, you will almost certainly need some help on the day with this type of reception. Some food simply cannot be prepared in advance; the rest will need reheating, thawing or arranging. It then needs to be served.

This can be done by plating up in the kitchen and using helpers to carry in the finished plates, or by handing the food round at the table. This really means waitresses who are experienced in 'silver service' and they will cost more than ordinary waitresses. Finally, there is the clearing away and washing-up to be taken care of.

# THE RECIPES

# TURKEY

After salmon, roast turkey is the next most popular choice for a cold buffet, perhaps with a matching roast ham. It is also a good choice for a hot sit-down meal. When you are ordering your bird make sure that it will fit into your oven. Your butcher will be able to give you an idea of the possible dimensions of a 5kg or 8kg turkey. Remember, there is quite a lot of bone in a turkey, so allow about 300g of meat per person. This means that a 6kg bird will serve about 20 people on its own or 30–45 with a good size ham roast.

## ROAST TURKEY

These timings are for a 6kg bird.

1. Wash and dry the turkey and place the stuffing in the neck end. Preheat the oven to 230°C/450°F/Gas 8. Coat the bird with plenty of softened butter and then cover with 10 rashers of streaky bacon, making sure the breast and the drumsticks are well covered. Wrap loosely in foil and place in the oven.
2. Fast roast for 2 hours, then remove the foil. After a further 15 minutes, remove the bacon rashers. When the turkey breast is browned, check that the bird is cooked through. Use a carving fork to plunge into the breast and thighs. The juices should run clear. If there is any blood, cover with foil again and continue roasting until thoroughly cooked.
3. Do not try to carve the bird the moment it comes out of the oven. The meat is much easier to carve if it stands for a short

while. If it is to be served hot, cover with foil and leave to stand for at least 10 minutes. If it is to be served cold, leave to cool completely before carving.

**TIP**
Keep the crispy bacon from the top of the turkey to crumble into salads.

## WALNUT STUFFING

It is not always easy to know how much stuffing to make. This recipe is sufficient for a 5–6kg bird.

**100g walnuts, or pecan nuts**
**100g butter**
**2 large celery sticks, sliced and chopped**
**1 large onion, finely chopped**
**350g fresh breadcrumbs**
**Grated rind of 2 oranges**
**4 tbsp freshly chopped parsley**
**¼ tsp dried mixed herbs**
**Salt and freshly ground black pepper**
**2 small eggs, beaten**

1. Toast the walnuts or pecans under the grill and chop fairly finely.
2. Heat the butter in a pan and gently fry the celery and onion until soft.
3. Remove from the heat and stir in the chopped nuts, breadcrumbs, grated orange rind, eggs, herbs and seasoning. Mix well together.
4. Use to stuff the turkey.

# GIBLET GRAVY

**Serves 20**

Giblets make a really well-flavoured gravy which can easily be made the day before.

**2 large onions, sliced**
**4 tbsp cooking oil**
**2 large carrots, sliced**
**1 stick celery, sliced**
**Giblets and neck from the turkey**
**½ bottle red wine**
**1½ litres water or vegetable stock**
**3 tbsp Bisto or other gravy powder**
**100ml water**

1. Fry the onions in half the cooking oil over a high heat. After a minute or so, add the carrots and celery and brown well. Remove from the pan and keep on one side.
2. Add more oil and the giblets and neck. Fry these until brown. Return the vegetables to the pan and add the wine and stock. Bring to the boil and cook until the liquid has reduced by half.
3. Strain the liquid and remove all the fat. Mix the Bisto with water and add to the liquid to thicken.
4. Return to the boil and cook for 3 minutes before serving.

# CREAM OF PUMPKIN SOUP

Pumpkins are very much part of Thanksgiving in the US and bonfire night in the UK, and this recipe gives a festive boost to this humble vegetable.

**Serves 16**

150ml olive oil
2 large onions, chopped
500g carrots, peeled and cut into thick slices
1kg pumpkin, peeled and cut into chunks
3 litres vegetable stock
500ml orange juice
Grated zest of 2 large oranges
1 x 4cm piece fresh root ginger, grated
300ml double cream
Salt and freshly ground black pepper

1. Heat the olive oil in a large saucepan, add the chopped onion and cook slowly until soft but without browning in colour. Stir from time to time.
2. Add the carrots and pumpkin, cover the pan and cook at a moderate heat for 10 minutes, stirring from time to time.
3. Add the vegetable stock. Cover and continue cooking for about 30 minutes until the vegetables are soft.
4. Purée the soup in a food processor. Return the mixture to the pan and mix with the orange juice and zest, grated ginger, cream, salt and pepper.
5. Serve at once.

# GRILLED PEPPER RAMEKINS WITH HOUMOUS

The longer you can leave these ramekins in the fridge the better they will keep their shape when you come to turn them out. However, the flavour is just as good whatever shape they are in! Serve with toasted ciabatta or French bread.

**Serves 12**

**12 large red or mixed coloured peppers, seeded and cut into quarters**
**24 tbsp houmous**
**24 large sprigs fresh basil**
**Salt and freshly ground black pepper**
**Extra virgin olive oil**

1. Place the pieces of pepper skin-side up under a hot grill and cook until well seared. It is not necessary to remove the skin, but if you have time you may prefer to do so.
2. Line 12 small ramekin dishes with pieces of pepper.
3. Place a spoonful of houmous in each one and top with basil leaves and seasoning. Cover with more pepper pieces and repeat the houmous, basil and seasoning layer. Finish off with a final layer of peppers.
4. Cover with cling film and place in the fridge until required.
5. Turn out to serve on individual plates and decorate with more basil leaves. Drizzle with extra virgin olive oil and serve at once.

# CHILLED SEAFOOD SOUP

This soup is even more classy than Vichyssoise. Serve it as a light starter.

**Serves 12**

1 tbsp olive oil
Knob of butter
1 small onion, sliced
1 leek, trimmed and sliced
1 carrots, peeled and diced
2 small potatoes, peeled and diced
200g white fish fillets (cod, whiting or huss), skinned and boned
1.25 litres fish stock, made with boiling water and 4 fish
   stock cubes
2 bay leaves
200g peeled prawns
250ml double cream
Salt and freshly ground black pepper
6 tbsp finely chopped chives, for decoration

1. Heat the olive oil in a pan with the butter and gently fry the onion and leek for 2–3 minutes. Add the carrots and potatoes and continue frying for a further 3–4 minutes, but do not allow the vegetables to brown.
2. Add the white fish, stock and bay leaves and bring to the boil. Cover with a lid and simmer for 25 minutes.
3. Remove the bay leaves and purée in a blender with the prawns or rub through a sieve. Leave to cool and then chill for 1 hour.
4. Stir in the cream and season to taste. Serve sprinkled with the chives.

# POMME D'AMOUR EGGS

This is quite an easy dish to prepare for large numbers.

**Serves 60**

4 x 25g packets aspic jelly
45 large eggs
75ml milk
100g butter
Salt and freshly ground black pepper
1.25kg smoked salmon, chopped
60 large tomatoes

*Decoration*
6–7 gem lettuces, slit into individual leaves
1 cucumber, sliced
2 bunches freshly chopped parsley
A little freshly chopped tarragon

1. Make up the aspic jelly as directed on the pack and leave to set in 2 Swiss roll tins.
2. Scramble the eggs, milk and butter in four equal batches. Season with salt and pepper and leave to cool. Stir in the smoked salmon.
3. Cut the tomatoes in half around the middle, scoop out the centres and pulp with a spoon. Sprinkle with salt.
4. Chop the aspic finely.
5. Spoon some of the scrambled egg mixture into each tomato half and place two halves on each plate.
6. Garnish the plate with chopped aspic, lettuce leaves and cucumber slices. Mix together the chopped parsley and tarragon and sprinkle over the top.

# FENNEL AND AVOCADO SALAD

Presentation is the essence of this dish, so try to make it as pretty as possible. Use small baking rings to place the fennel salad and arrange the slices of avocado in a fan shape.

**Serves 30**

**12 medium-sized heads of fennel, trimmed**
**3 red peppers, seeded and cut into thin slivers**
**1 cucumber, very finely diced**
**12 avocados, peeled and sliced**
**50ml fresh lemon juice**

*Decoration*
**Sprouted alfalfa**
**Pomegranate seeds**

*Dressing*
**450ml walnut oil**
**100ml fresh lemon juice**
**Salt and freshly ground black pepper**

1. Cut the heads of fennel in half and place in a large pan of boiling water. Cook for about 10 minutes until the fennel has softened but is still firm to the bite or al dente. Drain and leave to cool.
2. Finely chop the cooked fennel and mix with the slivers of red pepper and diced cucumber. Place a spoonful of the mixture in a small mountain on each plate.
3. Peel and slice the avocados and place in a bowl. Pour over the lemon juice and toss gently together.
4. Arrange the slices of avocado on each plate with the fennel salad in a small fan shape. Finish the plate with alfalfa and scattered pomegranate seeds.
5. Finally, mix the dressing ingredients with a fork and drizzle over the salads.

# SMOKED SALMON PARCELS
# WITH PRAWNS

This is an easy dish to prepare in advance and store in the fridge until required.

**Serves 20**

750g thin-cut smoked salmon
600g small prawns
350g cream cheese
5cm cucumber, very finely chopped
5 small spring onions, very finely chopped
Salt and freshly ground black pepper
Very thin slices of lemon, for garnish

1. Use the smoked salmon to line 20 small ramekin dishes (base approx. 7cm), leaving sufficient salmon overhanging the sides to cover the top in due course.
2. Mix the prawns with the cream cheese, cucumber and spring onions and season to taste. Spoon into the prepared ramekin dishes and fold the smoked salmon over the top. Store in the fridge until required.
3. Turn out the parcels onto small serving plates and garnish with very thin slices of lemon folded into a fan shape. Serve at once.

# ITALIAN STUFFED PEPPERS

It is important to ensure that the peppers are cooked through. There should still be plenty of juices in the pan at the end of the cooking time as these are an integral part of the dish. If the juices with the peppers show signs of drying up, add some more olive oil and wine and continue cooking until the peppers are tender.

**Serves 20**

10 large red peppers
Salt and freshly ground black pepper
5 cloves garlic, peeled and sliced
20 anchovy fillets
10 medium tomatoes
300ml extra virgin olive oil
300ml white wine
Rocket, for garnish

1. Preheat the oven to 200°C/400°F/Gas 6.
2. Start by cutting the peppers in half, through the stalks if possible. Remove all the seeds and fibres and arrange cut-side up in roasting tins. Season inside each pepper and place a slice of garlic and an anchovy in each one.
3. Cut the tomatoes in half round the centres and place one half in each pepper half. Pour a tablespoon of olive oil into each half. Pour the wine into the base of the roasting tins.
4. Cover with foil and bake for about 35–40 minutes, removing the foil about 10 minutes before the end of cooking time. Test the peppers to see that they are cooked through.
5. To serve, place a half pepper on each plate, sharing out the juices between all the plates. Finally, garnish with rocket and serve at once with crusty French bread or ciabatta to mop up the juices.

# RAINBOW ROULADES

Beg, borrow or steal five Swiss roll tins to make this colourful roulade, which tastes just as good as it looks. A good vegetarian option, these roulades also make unusual starters for non-vegetarian meals.

**Serves 30**

1.25kg carrots, peeled and chopped
Salt and freshly ground black pepper
225g butter
225g plain flour
900ml milk
15 eggs, separated

*Filling*
1kg quark or low-fat soft cheese
700g frozen chopped spinach, thawed and drained
¼ tsp nutmeg
Salt and pepper

1. Preheat the oven to 190°C/375°F/Gas 5 and line five 28 x 20cm Swiss roll tins with non-stick baking paper.
2. Cook the carrots in a little salted boiling water for about 10 minutes. Drain and mash well with a potato masher.
3. Place the butter, flour and milk in a saucepan and slowly bring to the boil, whisking all the time. The sauce should be quite thick. Stir in the carrots and season to taste, then add the egg yolks.

4. Whisk the egg whites until they are very stiff and add a tablespoonful to the carrot mixture.

5. Fold in the rest of the whites. Spread the mixture smoothly over the prepared Swiss roll tins and bake for 25 minutes.

6. Prepare the filling by mixing the quark or soft cheese with the spinach, nutmeg and seasoning. Spoon into a pan and heat gently.

7. Cover a wire rack with a tea towel and turn out one of the cooked roulades onto this. Immediately remove the paper and spread with some of the hot filling. Holding the tea towel in both hands, gently roll up the roulade like a Swiss roll.

8. Repeat with the remaining four roulades. Serve hot, sliced into rounds.

# SPINACH AND CHESTNUT FILO PIE

This vegetarian filo pie is rather special. The unusual filling is based on a southern Italian recipe for a pasta filling, but it works just as well in filo pastry. Look for canned roast chestnut purée, which has a particularly good flavour, but any kind of unsweetened chestnut purée will do. I usually use cream cheese, but if you prefer a lower fat content or do not want to use dairy food at all then silken tofu also works very well. The pie can be served as a first course or as a main with a salad or vegetables

**Serves 24**

**Extra virgin olive oil**
**18 sheets filo pastry**

*Filling*
**1.5kg fresh leaf spinach**
**750g tub cream, curd or ricotta cheese, or silken tofu**
**3 x 435g tins roast chestnut purée**
**Juice and grated rind of 2 small lemons**
**3 tsp dried thyme or oregano**
**3 tsp coriander seeds, crushed**
**Salt and freshly ground black pepper**

1. Preheat the oven to 200°C/400°F/Gas 6 and brush three 27 x 17cm Swiss roll tins with olive oil.
2. Steam the spinach with very little water until it begins to wilt. Drain well and keep to one side.

3. Mix the cheese or tofu with the chestnut purée, lemon juice and rind, herbs and spices and seasoning. It should form a smooth creamy paste.

4. Line each Swiss roll tin with three layers of filo pastry, brushing each layer with olive oil as you go. Spoon the chestnut mixture into the base and then spread the spinach over the top.

5. Cover with three more layers of oil-brushed filo.

6. Cut each one into eight squares with a sharp knife. Place in the oven and bake for 15 minutes. Serve at once.

## VARIATIONS

For a subtle oriental flavour, substitute 2–3 tablespoons of soy sauce for the lemon juice and add a pinch of five-spice powder.

# BOEUF EN CROUTE

Sometimes known as Beef Wellington, this super wedding breakfast special can be semi-prepared the day before. Store in the fridge overnight. Order the fillet in advance from the butcher, but if you cannot find a really large fillet, use two smaller ones instead and cook for 20–25 minutes only. It is a good idea to practise this dish once to see how long it actually takes to cook the meat to your taste.

**Serves 12**

1 x 2.25kg fillet of beef
50g unsalted butter, softened
Plain flour, for rolling out
450g puff pastry, fresh or frozen and thawed
1 x 75g tin pâté de foie or any kind of smooth pâté
½ tsp dried thyme
Salt and freshly ground black pepper
1 egg, beaten

1. Preheat the oven to 220°C/425°F/Gas 7.
2. Trim any fat from the fillet and roll into a neat shape; tie at intervals with string. Spread the softened butter over the top, place in a baking tin and bake for 10 minutes. Remove the fillet from the oven and leave to cool. It is essential to allow the cooked fillet to go completely cold before wrapping in pastry.

3.  Roll the pastry out on a floured surface/board to an 8mm-thick oblong three times the width of the fillet, retaining any trimmings. Spread the pâté over the top of the fillet and place the fillet, pâté-side down, on the pastry. Sprinkle the fillet with thyme and salt and pepper.

4.  Fold the pastry over the meat and seal the seam with a little water. Turn the whole thing over so that the join is underneath. Prick the top with a fork and decorate with any leftover pastry. Place on a board and leave in the fridge for 1 hour.

5.  To cook the fillet, place on a wet baking tray. Brush the top and sides with beaten egg and bake again at 220°C/425°F/Gas 7 for 25–35 minutes, until the pastry is well browned and the meat is cooked to your taste.

# CHICKEN IN TARRAGON CREAM SAUCE

Chicken is a good choice of meat if you are not sure whether you need to make any special dietary considerations in the way of meat for your guests. It also has the advantage of being relatively economical. Jointing five chickens is quite a task, so ask your butcher to cut the backbone from the chickens and to cut each one into eight pieces. Use the bones from the chicken to make a good stock.

**Serves 20**

**5 x 1.5kg chickens**
**125g plain flour**
**Salt and freshly ground black pepper**
**75ml olive oil**
**750ml white wine**
**750ml chicken stock**
**2 small onions, peeled and left whole**
**4 tbsp dried tarragon**
**500ml single cream**
**50g butter**

1. Cut each chicken into four joints, removing the backbone (use this to make stock). Skin the joints and cut each joint in half to give eight pieces per chicken. For a more elegant result, remove any bones still adhering to the pieces of breast.
2. Mix 75g flour with salt and pepper and toss the chicken pieces in this mixture.

3. Heat the oil in a large frying pan and fry the chicken pieces in batches until lightly browned. Transfer to a large heavy-based pan. Add the white wine, stock, onions and half the tarragon. Cover and cook over a low heat until the chicken is cooked through.

4. Discard the onions. Drain off all the cooking liquor into another saucepan and reduce over a high heat to about two-thirds. Remove from the heat and stir in the cream and the rest of the tarragon.

5. Mix the remaining flour with the butter to make a thick paste and add to the pan in very small pieces, whisking all the time. Continue whisking until the mixture thickens. Correct the seasoning.

6. Arrange the chicken on large platters and pour on the tarragon cream sauce.

# BEEF IN RED WINE

It takes quite a long time to cut up, flour and fry off the meat for this recipe, so try and get some help for this stage of the preparation. The advantage of the recipe is that there is nothing to do on the day except to reheat it. For smaller numbers simply scale down the quantities, allowing a little more liquid proportionally.

**Serves 60**

10kg chuck steak, cut into chunks
150–200g plain flour
Salt and freshly ground black pepper
Olive oil
1.2 litres red wine
2kg onions, sliced
450g leeks, trimmed and sliced
6 cloves garlic, peeled and chopped
1kg carrots, peeled and sliced
2 bouquets garnis
3 litres beef stock
Cornflour or gravy powder (optional)
1kg button mushrooms

1.  Toss the meat in the flour seasoned with salt and pepper and fry in olive oil in batches in a large frying pan until well browned. Transfer to one or two large casserole pots. After you have finished frying the meat, de-glaze the pan by pouring in half of the red wine and bring to the boil, stirring all the time. Pour over the meat.

2. Fry the onions, leeks, garlic and carrots in more olive oil in a clean pan until lightly browned. Add to the meat with the bouquets garnis and stir well. De-glaze the pan again with another 600ml red wine. Add to the meat.

3. Pour in the remaining red wine and add sufficient beef stock to barely cover the meat. Cover and bake at 160°C/325°F/ Gas 3 for 2 hours.

4. Stir and check the thickness of the juices. If they are a little thin, thicken with a tablespoon of cornflour or gravy powder dissolved in cold water. Stir into the casserole with the button mushrooms and continue cooking for a further 2 hours.

# FENNEL IN CREAM SAUCE

This way of serving vegetables also works very well with celeriac.

**Serves 20**

**10 large heads of fennel, trimmed and sliced**
**500ml double cream**
**1 tbsp potato or cornflour**
**300ml chicken stock**
**500ml white wine**
**Salt and freshly ground black pepper**

1. Cook the fennel in a steamer or in a pan with a very small quantity of water until tender. Transfer to a shallow entrée dish.
2. To make the cream sauce, mix 3 tablespoons of the double cream with the potato or cornflour to make a smooth cream and keep on one side.
3. Pour the remaining cream, chicken stock and white wine into a pan and bring to the boil. Continue boiling fast until the mixture has thickened somewhat.
4. Remove from the heat and stir in the cream and flour mix and whisk well together. Return to the boil and cook again until the sauce reaches a good creamy consistency. Season and pour over the cooked fennel.

# TIA MARIA CREAMS

This Tia Maria flavoured cream goes beautifully with the ginger tones of the Brandy Snaps (pages 258–9). It is best to make this dessert at the last minute.

**Serves 20**

3 tbsp instant coffee
600ml water
250ml Tia Maria
300g Barbados (muscovado) sugar
2 litres double cream
20 brandy snaps

1. Dissolve the coffee in the water and stir well.
2. Place the mixture in a bowl with the Tia Maria and sugar, and stir again until the sugar has dissolved.
3. Pour in the double cream and whisk with an electric whisk until the mixture thickens and remains in soft peaks.
4. Spoon into individual sundae dishes and serve at once with brandy snaps.

# PASSION FRUIT PAVLOVA

I have it on good authority from an Australian friend that this is the traditional filling for the ever-popular meringue case. The prepared pavlova base can be kept in a tin or frozen for several weeks.

**Serves 12**

6 egg whites (size 3)
350g caster sugar
4 papaya fruit, peeled, seeded and sliced
6 passion fruit, cut in half
600ml double cream
1 tsp vanilla essence

1. Preheat the oven to 140°C/275°F/Gas 1. Draw a 25cm diameter circle on a sheet of non-stick or greaseproof paper and place on a flat metal baking sheet.
2. Whisk the egg whites until stiff, then gradually add the sugar, whisking between each addition.
3. Spoon half tablespoons of the meringue on to the paper and spread out to fill the circle. Pipe the remaining meringue in two or three rings on top of each other around the edge to form a case.
4. Bake for 1 hour. Leave to cool and then carefully remove the paper.
5. Purée three of the papaya fruit with the pulp from the passion fruit. Whisk the cream with the vanilla until soft peaks are formed and fold in the fruit purée.
6. Spoon into the centre of the meringue case and decorate with slices of the remaining papaya.

# SLICED STRAWBERRIES
# WITH ROMANOFF CREAM

If you prefer to make your own meringues, use the recipe for Passion Fruit Pavlova on the previous page.

**Serves 60**

4.5kg strawberries
3 litres double cream
225g caster sugar
75ml kirsch
40 medium meringues, broken up

1. Wash and dry the strawberries, then remove the leaves and slice.
2. Mix the cream, sugar and kirsch together and beat with a wire whisk to thicken to the soft-peak stage.
3. Just before serving, fold in the broken meringues and then the strawberries. Spoon into a large glass bowl and decorate with a few more strawberries.

# LEMON TARTS

Buy ready-made puff or flaky pastry for these delicious little tarts. Even better if you can find them, use ready-rolled pastry sheets.

**Makes 20**

**250g puff or flaky pastry**
**Plain flour, for rolling out**

*Filling*
**4 lemons**
**6 eggs**
**250g sugar**
**100g butter, just melted**

1. Preheat the oven to 190°C/375°F/Gas 5 and oil two 12-bun or tart trays.
2. Roll out the pastry on a floured surface if necessary and cut out 24 rounds to line the bun or tart trays.
3. Grate the zest from one of the lemons and squeeze the juice from all four lemons; keep on one side.
4. Beat the eggs and sugar together with a whisk and then stir in the lemon zest and juice. Finally, beat in the melted butter.
5. Spoon the mixture into the pastry-lined bun or tart trays and bake immediately for 15–20 minutes, taking care not to overcook.

# PISTACHIO NUT FUDGE

This is a rather unusual fudge, which is fun to serve at the end of a meal with the coffee.

**Makes about 1lb**

350g granulated sugar
75ml water
1 x 410g tin condensed milk
50g butter, plus extra for greasing
50g pistachio kernels
Seeds from 3 cardamom pods, crushed

1. Butter or oil a small 18cm square tin.
2. Put the sugar and water in a pan with the milk and butter and heat slowly, stirring until the sugar has dissolved. Raise the heat and bring the mixture to the boil. Continue boiling until the mixture reaches the soft ball stage or 113°C/235°F.
3. Remove the pan from the heat and dip the base in cold water. Add the nuts and crushed seeds and beat the fudge with a wooden spoon. When it beings to stiffen, pour into the prepared tin. Mark the top into squares with the point of a knife and leave to cool.
4. When completely cool cut into squares and store in an airtight tin.

# BRANDY SNAPS

These crunchy curls can be filled with whipped cream or crème patissière, but this must be done at the last minute or the brandy snaps will lose their crunch and go soft. Arrange on a platter with Mini-Meringues (page 149) and Chocolate-iced Cupcakes (page 153) and serve with the coffee.

**Makes 30**

150g butter
150g caster sugar
6 tbsp (heaped dollops) golden syrup
150g plain flour
3 tsp ground ginger
3 tsp brandy
3 tsp grated lemon rind

1. Preheat the oven to 180°C/350°F/Gas 4 and line a large baking tray with baking paper – you can grease with just a little oil instead, but it's more difficult to time exactly when to lift the cooked biscuits.
2. Place the butter, sugar and syrup in a pan and stir over a gentle heat. When the butter and sugar have melted, stir in all the remaining ingredients. Leave to cool a little.
3. Place 2–3 spoonfuls onto the baking tray, well apart, and bake for 5–7 minutes until light brown in the centre and the rest is darker brown and lacy. Remove from the oven and leave to cool a little.

4. Lift off the biscuits with a fish slice and shape into curls or cigar shapes using a wooden spoon handle. You can also shape over narrow-based breakfast cups to make tulips to fill with ice cream or fruit. Either way, place on a wire rack to cool.

5. Continue cooking in batches. Do not let the uncooked mixture stiffen too much or later biscuits will not spread enough.

**TIPS**

Here are the secrets of successful brandy snaps. They can be quite difficult to make, so try a dry run the week before:

- Make sure the mixture is runny enough to spread
- Ensure there is plenty of room on the tray
- Leave for a minute or so before attempting to remove from the tray and curl up – critical!
- Leave on the wooden spoon handle for 3 or 4 minutes or they will collapse in the middle

# INDEX